Killis Campbell

A Study of the Romance of the Seven Sages

With Special Reference to the Middle English Versions

Killis Campbell

A Study of the Romance of the Seven Sages
With Special Reference to the Middle English Versions

ISBN/EAN: 9783744695862

Printed in Europe, USA, Canada, Australia, Japan

Cover: Foto ©Thomas Meinert / pixelio.de

More available books at **www.hansebooks.com**

A STUDY OF THE ROMANCE OF THE SEVEN SAGES WITH SPECIAL REFERENCE TO THE MIDDLE ENGLISH VERSIONS

A DISSERTATION

PRESENTED TO THE BOARD OF UNIVERSITY STUDIES
OF THE JOHNS HOPKINS UNIVERSITY FOR THE
DEGREE OF DOCTOR OF PHILOSOPHY

BY

KILLIS CAMPBELL

FORMERLY FELLOW IN ENGLISH AT THE JOHNS HOPKINS UNIVERSITY

BALTIMORE
THE MODERN LANGUAGE ASSOCIATION OF AMERICA
1898

JOHN MURPHY & CO., PRINTERS,
BALTIMORE.

[Reprinted from the *Publications of the Modern Language Association of America*, Vol. XIV, No. 1.]

TABLE OF CONTENTS.

		PAGE.
A Word of Introduction,		1
I. The Earlier History of the Romance,		3
I (a).	The Romance in the Orient,	3
I (b).	Transmission of the Romance to the Occident,	12
I (c).	The Romance in France and Italy,	20
	1. The *Dolopathos*,	21
	2. The *Sept Sages de Rome*,	24
II. The Romance in England,		35
II (a).	The Middle English Versions,	37
	1. Description of the Manuscripts,	37
	2. Interrelation of the Middle English Versions,	43
	3. Authorship of the Middle English Versions,	84
	4. Source of the Middle English Versions,	87
II (b).	Sixteenth Century and Chap-book Versions,	91
Appendix,		94

A STUDY OF THE ROMANCE OF THE SEVEN SAGES WITH SPECIAL REFERENCE TO THE MIDDLE ENGLISH VERSIONS.

A Word of Introduction.

The main object of this study has been to investigate thoroughly the relations of the Middle English versions of the *Seven Sages of Rome*.

As preliminary to this investigation, a review of the history of the romance in the several stages through which it has passed before reaching English has been made. This survey, a recapitulation of the results which modern scholarship has attained in the study of the romance, has been made impartially, and with a view to set forth the most approved views that have been held rather than to advance any new theories of my own. Where these views are conflicting, as is particularly the case with respect to the eastern versions, I have endeavored to sift truth from error, though here naturally some difficulty has been encountered. It is only on the question of transmission of the romance that a view differing from that of the best authorities has been taken.

The chapter on the French and the Italian versions has been based in large part on the work of Gaston Paris, whose *Deux*

Rédactions has superseded all previous contributions, representing as it does the most recent and the best results that have been attained in this branch of the study of the romance. Additions which have been made consist largely in information as to a number of manuscripts which were unknown to Paris, or which have since been found.

The second and major part of the study has been devoted to the *Seven Sages* in English. Here I have been preceded by Petras and Buchner, the one dealing mainly with the Middle English group, the other especially with the relations of the Wynkyn de Worde and Rolland versions. The dissertations of these two scholars are the only real contributions which have been made to the study of the English versions. It is therefore not surprising that many of the current theories with regard to these versions are shown on closer examination to be erroneous. The most far-reaching of these misconceptions is, I believe, that which regards the Wright version as independent of all other English versions. My investigations lead me to the conviction that at least seven of the eight Middle English manuscripts are related to each other through a common Middle English original.

I regret that I have been forced to forego consideration of one of the Middle English versions,—the Asloan. I was denied access to this manuscript by its owner, Lord Talbot de Malahide, and learned of the existence of a transcript of it in the University Library at Edinburgh when it was too late to avail myself of it. Prof. Varnhagen believes it to have had an immediate basis on some Old French manuscript; there are reasonable grounds for doubting this belief, however, and I am unwilling to subscribe to it until a further comparison with the remaining Middle English versions has been made.

This study leaves undone the most interesting, if not the most valuable part of the work I had planned,—a comparative study of the stories themselves; for not even the stories of the *Bidpai* collection have enjoyed a wider vogue than those of the *Seven Sages*. The task of tracing these in their travels and of collecting their analogues will be attempted in a future publication, when it is hoped that an edition of one or more of the unpublished Middle English manuscripts may also be attempted.

I. THE EARLIER HISTORY OF THE ROMANCE.

I (a). *The Romance in the Orient.*

It is universally held to-day that the great collection of popular stories known in the West as the *Seven Sages of Rome*, in the East as the *Book of Sindibād*, is of Indian origin. This was well established by Deslongchamps already in 1838, in his *Essai sur les Fables Indiennes*,[1] and has never since been seriously brought in question. The Indian original, however, has not yet been discovered, nor is it probable that it ever will be; and it even admits of very considerable doubt whether the romance ever existed in India in a form very near to that in which it is first found.

All attempts, too, to show a kinship between the romance and some surviving Sanskrit story have proved in large part futile. Benfey first pointed out the analogy between the introduction to the *Pantchatantra* and the framework of the *Sindibād*,[2] but he very justly concluded that the *Pantchatantra* was indebted to the *Sindibād* rather than the *Sindibād* to the *Pantchatantra*. In a later publication,[3] he called attention to the similarity between the *Sindibād* and the legend of Kunāla and Asoka, and Cassel has boldly assumed this legend to be the ultimate basis of the romance.[4]

The story of Kunāla is widely known in Sanskrit literature. Asoka, a famous Indian king, had, after the death of his first wife, married one of the latter's attendants. The

---
[1] Published at Paris, 1838, in conjunction with Leroux de Lincy's edition of the *Sept Sages de Rome*.
[2] *Pantchatantra*, Leipzig, 1859, I, § 8; also *Mélanges Asiat.*, III, p. 188 f.
[3] *Orient and Occident*, III, p. 177 f.
[4] *Mischle Sindbad*, Berlin, 1888, pp. 10 f., 62.

new queen had been rejected previous to this by Kunāla, the son of Asoka by another wife, and bore in consequence the greatest hatred toward him. The prince is sent by Asoka to one of the provinces to put down a rebellion, where he wins great distinction for himself. In the meantime the king is stricken with a fatal disease, and determines to recall the young prince and place him on the throne. The queen, realizing what this would mean to her, offers to cure the king provided he grant her one favor. Having been restored to health through her agency, the king agrees to grant her whatever she may desire. She asks to be permitted to exercise supreme authority for seven days, during which time, at her instigation, the prince's beautiful eyes[1] are put out. Kunāla subsequently presents himself before his father in the guise of a lute-player, and is recognized. The queen is burned in expiation of her crime.[2]

Such in brief outline is the legend, which, if it is indeed the ultimate origin of the *Sindibād*, at least does not suggest an obvious relation to it.

Abundant proof of a Sanskrit origin of the *Sindibād*, however, is had in the nature or content of its stories and, in particular, of its framework, which is distinctly Buddhistic. Cassel has treated this aspect of the problem at great length.[3] He would concede as the result of his investigations that some of the many varying stories were not found in the hypothetical original, and that no one of the extant versions faithfully represents this original. Nor is it strange that this should be the case, for it would be a very miracle had the collection remained intact throughout a possible half-dozen redactions. It is, accordingly, impossible to determine which of the stories were in the original, or which not; this, for the present at least, must remain largely a matter of conjecture. Still, this

---

[1] Cf. *Mischle Sindbad*, p. 10.
[2] For further details of this legend, see Burnouf, *Introduction à l'histoire du Buddhisme indien*, Paris, 1844, pp. 144 f., 406.
[3] *Mischle Sindbad*, p. 82 f.

much may be accepted as established, that some of the original stories, the ethical purpose, and many of the general characteristics of the Indian prototype have been preserved.

The Eastern group comprises a Hebrew, a Syriac, a Greek, an Old Spanish, two closely related and a third somewhat anomalous Persian, and three cognate Arabic versions. All these differ more or less from each other, but, as compared with the Western group, with which they have in common only four stories and the framework, they distinctly stand apart and make up a separate group. There are many important details in which the two groups differ, but the most marked features which characterize the Eastern group are, first, that each sage tells *two* tales as against *one* each in the western versions[1]—a feature which was probably not in the Sanskrit original; and, secondly, in contradistinction to the entire western group with the exception of the *Dolopathos*, that the prince has only one instructor, the philosopher Sindibād. This illustrious teacher is the central figure of all versions in the East, where by general consent the romance is called after him the *Book of Sindibād*.[2]

The origin of the name *Sindibād* is in dispute. Benfey traces it back to *Siddhapatī,[3] Teza to *Siddhapala;[4] Cassel, on the contrary, holds that the word was coined first after leaving India, and is neither *Siddhapatī* nor *Siddhapala*, but *Sindubadhjāja = Indian teacher.[5]

The name of the prince has not been preserved, but the king is named in each one of the representative eastern texts. In the Syriac and the Greek he is called *Kurus;* in the Old

---

[1] This is the case in all eastern versions save the *Seven Vezirs* and the version of Nachshebī: in the former some sages tell one, some two stories; in the latter each sage tells only one.

[2] Prof. Rhys Davids in his work on the *Jātakas* (*Buddhist Birth Stories*, Boston, 1880, vol. I, pp. XLI, XCIV) seems to have confounded this romance with the story of *Sinbad the Sailor* of the *Arabian Nights*. The two are in no way related.

[3] *Pantchatantra*, I, § 5 (p. 23).

[4] *Il Libro dei Sette Savj*, ed. D'Ancona, Pisa, 1864, p. XLVII.

[5] *Mischle Sindbad*, p. 66.

Spanish, *Alcos*, which may be considered a variant of *Kurus* (*Al-Curus*), since the Spanish holds very closely with the Greek and Syriac, and goes back to the same original. The Hebrew version, on the other hand, calls the king *Pai Pur*, or, as Benfey has suggested, *Kai* (king) *Pur*, and Cassel would identify this Pur with the Indian king Porus, ruler of India at the time of the Alexandrian invasion, and third before King Asoka of the Kunāla story. Porus, Cassel maintains, is a substitution for the less famous Asoka of the original—a transference of the Asoka tradition to Porus.[1] The Kurus of the Greek and Syriac he would explain in like manner as a similar transference, after leaving India, from Porus, or Asoka, to the far-famed Cyrus of the Persians.[2]

The route of transmission from India westward is very generally assumed to have been through Pahlavī into Arabic.[3] There seems to be little evidence, however, of the existence of a Pahlavī version, unless the current tradition to that effect, or the fact that the *Kalila wa Dimna* had such an intermediate stage, be regarded as such. Hence Cassel takes a radically different view from that generally held, maintaining that the lost Arabic text goes back not to a Pahlavī but to a Syriac version, which, in its turn, goes back to the Sanskrit,—the collection, then, having been transmitted westward through the agency of the Manicheans in the third or fourth century of our era.[4] The Hebrew and the lost Arabic versions he conceives to be coördinate redactions of this early Syriac version, finding support of this theory, so far as it concerns the Hebrew text, in the Syriac influence which the language of the latter exhibits. At the same time, although he thus claims for the Hebrew version the greatest antiquity of any text which has been preserved, Cassel admits that, in addition to the Syriac influence, the Hebrew text also contains traces of a Greek influence (as, for instance, in the names of the

---

[1] *Ibid.*, pp. 63, 212.   [2] *Ibid.*, p. 61.
[3] So Comparetti, Nöldeke, Clouston, and others.
[4] *Mischle Sindbad*, pp. 61, 310.

sages),[1] which is of itself sufficiently indicative of the lack of conclusive proof of his thesis.[2] The Arabic text, unlike the early Syriac, is in no way hypothetical, but the evidence that it once existed, even as late as the thirteenth century,[3] is conclusive. Its influence has been very wide, and, until Cassel, it has been generally assumed to be the source, either mediate or immediate, of the entire Eastern group. The Syriac *Sindban* and the Old Spanish version are believed to be its closest representatives. Its author, according to the testimony of the introduction to the *Syntipas*, was a certain Musa, and its date has been conjecturally placed by Nöldeke[4] and others in the eighth century.

Only ten versions belonging to the Eastern type have survived. These are the Hebrew *Mischle Sindbad*, the Syriac *Sindban*, the Greek *Syntipas*, the Persian *Sindibād-nāmeh* and its source, the text of As-Samarquandī, the Old Spanish *Libro de los Engannos*, the three Arabic versions of the *Seven Vezirs*, and the eighth night of the *Tūtī-nāmeh* of Nachshebī.[5]

The relative age of these is not definitely known. Early scholars as a rule held that the Hebrew version antedated all others; but this view was summarily rejected by Comparetti[6] and his followers, who claimed greatest antiquity for the *Syntipas*, a distinction of which it was robbed by Rödiger's discovery of the Syriac version. The Nachshebī version has also been held to be the oldest,[7] and Clouston in recent years

[1] These are, according to Cassel (p. 219 f.), Sindibād, Hippocrates, Apuleius, Lucian, Aristotle, Pindar, and Homer.
[2] *Mischle Sindbad*, pp. 222, 310.
[3] The Old Spanish version was made from it in 1253.
[4] In his review of Baethgen's edition of the *Sindban* in *Zeitschrift d. d. Morg. Gesellschaft*, XXXIII, p. 518.
[5] All these, with the exception of the text of As-Samarquandī, have been rendered accessible either in the original or in translations, and in most cases in both.
[6] Comparetti, *Book of Sindibād*, p. 53 f. Citation is made from the English translation by Coote, for the *Folk Lore Socy.*, London, 1882. The original *Ricerche* appeared at Milan in 1869.
[7] Brockhaus for example.

has contended for the *Sindibād-nāmeh* as representing most closely the hypothetical original.[1] The result of the latest investigation, as has been seen, is to return to the view of early scholars, which gives to the Hebrew text first place both as regards date and fidelity to the lost original. Such is Cassel's conclusion, which, although somewhat revolutionary, is arrived at by argument which at least serves to invalidate Comparetti's assumption that the Hebrew text stands for a late and very free version of the romance. It is hardly legitimate to conclude, from the circumstance that the *Mischle Sindbad* stands apart from the remaining members of the Eastern group, that it is, on that account, less faithful to the original tradition. Nor is Comparetti's argument for the identification of the Joel to whom the work is attributed by Rossi and the British Museum manuscript, with the Joel who is reported to have translated the *Kalila wa Dimna* into Hebrew, and the consequent establishment of a thirteenth century date for this version, any more valid.[2] At the same time, it is to be regretted that Cassel has attained no definite results as to chronology.[3]

The *Mischle Sindbad*[4] contains twenty stories, three of which, *Absalom*, *The Disguised Youth*, and *The Humpbacks* (*amatores*), appear in no other version of the Eastern group. Its first three stories come in the same order as in the Syriac, Greek, and Old Spanish versions. Other agreements which are evident on reference to a comparative table serve apparently to hold these four texts together;[5] this, however, is probably rather due to a more faithful preservation of the

[1] Clouston, *Book of Sindibād* [Glasgow], 1884, p. L f.
[2] Comparetti, *Book of Sindibād*, p. 53 f.   [3] *Mischle Sindbad*, p. 310.
[4] The Hebrew text has undergone the following editions: Sengelman (with German translation), Halle, 1842; Carmoly (with French translation), Paris, 1849; and Cassel (German translation and copious notes), Berlin, 1888.
[5] For the most complete comparative table, see Landau, *Quellen des Dekameron*, 2d ed., Stuttgart, 1884; see also Cassel, p. 362 f., and Comparetti, p. 25.

ultimate original on the part of these than to any very close relationship with the Hebrew, and comparison will show not only that these three have much in common which does not appear in the Hebrew, but also that the latter has many features (the naming of the sages, for example) which are peculiarly its own. Additional importance attaches to the Hebrew text from the fact that it probably bears a closer relation to the Western group than any other known eastern version.[1]

The Syriac *Sindban* was discovered by Rödiger in 1866, and was published with a German translation by Baethgen in 1879.[2] The text is unfortunately fragmentary, especially at the end. Although at first doubted by Comparetti, it has been satisfactorily shown by Nöldeke to be the Syriac basis of the *Syntipas*, alluded to in the prologue of the latter.[3] The immediate original of the *Sindban* must then be the last Arabic text of Musa. Nöldeke believes it to belong to the tenth century.

The Greek *Syntipas* is, in interest and importance, second only to the Hebrew text. As compared with its Syriac original, it is much more full and ornate,—an almost unfailing characteristic of a later text. Its author was, as the prologue establishes, a certain Michael Andreopulos and the translation was made at the command of one Gabriel $\mu\epsilon\lambda\omega\nu\nu\mu\sigma$. Comparetti would identify this Gabriel with Duke Gabriel of Melitene, and thus establish the date of the work as the second half of the eleventh century;[4] but this, while a gain in a measure, is little more than a happy suggestion. Far less probability has Cassel's proposition that the reference is to the angel Gabriel.[5] The text was first published by

---

[1] See the next chapter on "The Transmission of the Romance to the Occident."
[2] Baethgen, *Sindban, oder die Sieben Weisen Meister*, Leipzig, 1879. An English translation by H. Gollancz appeared in *Folk Lore*, VIII, p. 99 f., June, 1897.
[3] *Zeitschr. d. d. Morg. Gesellschaft*, XXXIII, p. 513 f.
[4] *Book of Sindibâd*, p. 57.   [5] *Mischle Sindbad*, p. 368.

Boissonade, and has been lately critically edited by Eberhard.[1] A modern Greek adaptation of the older text is of little value in a comparative study of the romance.[2]

The *Libro de los Engannos*, like the Syriac text, was not known until late in the century. It is, according to its prologue, a translation from the Arabic, made in the year 1253. The text is complete, but very corrupt. Its closest affinities are with the Greek and Syriac versions, with both of which it exhibits intimate agreement in content and order of stories. It seems to have had no influence at all on modern Spanish literature. The first edition of the text appeared in Comparetti's *Ricerche*, in 1869; a second edition, with an admirable English translation appended, appeared in the English edition of this book in 1882.[3]

The Persian *Sindibād-nāmeh*[4] dates from the year 1375. It purports to be based on a Persian prose text which goes back to the Arabic. Clouston first suggested that this original was the text of As-Samarquandī, which was known in the early part of the century, but which had subsequently been lost sight of. By the rediscovery of a manuscript of this version in 1891, he has been enabled to establish this conjecture as a fact.[5] The As-Samarquandī text agrees closely with the *Sindibād-nāmeh* in content, the only important difference being the substitution on the part of the latter of one or two extraneous stories for those it found in its original. The agreement in order of stories is close throughout. The date of the prose text falls late in the twelfth century. It differs considerably from the rest of the Eastern group, but is nearer

---

[1] Eberhard, *Fabulae Romanenses Graece*, etc., I (Teubner), Leipzig, 1872.

[2] For the *Syntipas* in later literature, see Murko, "Die Geschichte v. d. Sieben Weisen b. d. Slaven," *Wiener Akad. Sitzungsb.*, Ph. Hist. Cl., CXXII, No. x, p. 4 f.

[3] *Book of Sindibād*, pp. 73–164.

[4] This text has not yet been edited. An abstract of it was given by Falconer in the *Asiatic Journal*, xxxv, p. 169 f. and xxxvi, pp. 4 f., 99 f.; a complete translation into English appears in Clouston's *Book of Sindibād*.

[5] *Athenaeum* for Sept. 12, 1891, p. 355.

to the Syriac, Greek and Spanish versions than to the Hebrew. There appears to be no evidence to support Clouston's suggestion that it represents the Sanskrit prototype more faithfully than any other known version; neither is Modi's contention for a close relation with the story of *Kaus, Sondābeh, and Siāvash*[1] by any means convincing; but the tradition which makes its origin in the Arabic text is doubtless well founded.

Under the head of the *Seven Vezirs* fall three versions which have been introduced into the frame of the *Arabian Nights*. These are the texts of Habicht and Scott, and the Boulaq edition.[2] They are of late composition, and of comparatively slight value for the present purpose.

The text contained in the eighth night of Nachshebī[3] is one of the most interesting of the Eastern group, and has given rise to much speculation. It differs considerably from all other related versions, having but six stories, only five of which appear elsewhere in the Eastern group. All five of these in the fuller versions are second vezir's tales, and as they were also found originally in the *Sukasaptatī* (though not connected as with Nachshebī), it has been conjectured by Comparetti that they were first introduced into the *Sindibād* after leaving India, and that Nachshebī, observing this, again inserted them in his free translation of the *Tūtī-nāmeh*, and practically in the same form in which he found them in the *Sindibād*.[4] Comparetti would further identify the collection before and after this addition with the 'Greater' and 'Lesser' *Sindibād* referred to by the tenth century Mohammed Ibn el Warrak. A radically different theory has been advanced by Nöldeke, who maintains that the 'Greater' *Sindibād* has been lost.[5] As for the version of the *Sindibād* whence Nachshebī

---

[1] Modi, *Dante and Viraf and Gardis and Kaus*, Bombay, 1892.
[2] *1001 Nights*, Breslau, 1840, xv, pp. 102–172; Scott, *Tales, Anecdotes and Letters*, Shrewsbury, 1800, p. 38 f.; *1001 Nights*, Boulaq, 1863, III, pp. 75–124.
[3] Brockhaus, *Nachshebī's S. W. M.*, Leipzig, 1845; translated by Teza, D'Ancona ed. of *Sette Savj.*, p. XXXVII f.
[4] *Book of Sindibād*, p. 37 f.
[5] *Zeitschr. d. d. Morg. Gesellschaft*, XXXIII, p. 521 f.

drew, both Comparetti and Nöldeke concur in the belief that it was the text on which the *Sindibād-nāmeh* was based, or that of As-Samarquandī. The date of the Nachshebī version is late, as its author died in 1329.

Besides the ten versions catalogued above, the existence of certain others which have been lost is proved by sundry references from oriental writers. A Persian text is attributed to Azrakī by Daulat Shāh, and there are several references from the ninth and tenth centuries to works which do not seem to be identical with anything which has been preserved. The best-known of these, probably, is Masūdī's (943) statement that in the reign of Kūrūsh "lived es-Sondbad, who is the author of the book of the seven vezirs, the teacher and boy, and the wife of the king. This is the book which bears the name *Kitāb-es-Sindbād*."[1] A still earlier reference is that of Al-Yaqūbī (880). Both of these may refer to the Arabic text of Musa, though this is by no means certain. Most perplexing of all is the reference, already mentioned, to a 'Greater' and a 'Lesser' *Book of Sindibād*.

Doubtless many more versions have been lost than this would indicate; but since nearly a third of the known texts have been revealed only within the last generation, it may be hoped that the near future has in store many revelations which will materially serve to dispel the mist which now surrounds almost the entire question of relations in the East.

I (*b*). *Transmission of the Romance to the Occident.*

The Greek *Syntipas* and the Old Spanish *Libro de los Engannos* are the only representatives of the Eastern group which have arisen on European territory. Neither one of these, however, can be considered a connecting link in the chain of transmission; nor can, in fact, with all certainty, any one member of the Eastern group claim this distinction.

---

[1] Masūdī, *Meadows of Gold*, translated by Sprenger, London, 1841, p. 175. Masūdī was not well acquainted with the romance, as follows from the fact that he attributes its authorship to Sindibād.

The question of transmission is, and must doubtless always remain, very much shrouded in darkness. The two groups, having in common only four stories and the framework, and having in these, also, many radical differences, cannot be thought of as connected through free or literal translation, nor by intermediate redactions; the only valid explanation of the enormous gap existing between them must repose in the assumption of a basis for the western original in popular tradition. This alone can explain the difference between the two groups.

But this assumption should not carry with it (as with Comparetti apparently; *l. c.*, p. 2) the further assumption that, since the medium of transmission was oral, all possibility of ever determining the specific original of the Western group is thereby done away with. This need not follow at all. The oral tradition on which the western parent version had its basis, must itself have had some basis, and this cannot have been the entire Eastern group, nor with any degree of probability any two of its members; it was some one member of the Eastern group. Accordingly it is legitimate to endeavor to determine which one of the Eastern versions is the original, or the closest representative of the original, of the Western group.

Modern scholars in general have refrained from any investigation of this stage of the history of the romance. With a single exception, the only judgments upon the problem date from the earlier part of the century. Dacier, Keller, Deslongchamps, Wright, D'Ancona, and others put forth claims for one or another of the Eastern group (some for the Greek, others for the Hebrew), as the original of the western type. But all these claims were unsustained by any evidence adduced, and were in every case scarcely more than conjectures. The modern scholar who alone has put himself on record here is Landau;[1] and he is, at the same time the only one of the

[1] Marcus Landau, *Quellen des Dekameron*, 2d ed., Stuttgart, 1884.

whole number who has made a serious effort to sustain his position. At the basis of Landau's work, however, lies the assumption that the Latin prose *Historia Septem Sapientum* (*H*) is the parent version of the Western group,—an assumption which is entirely gratuitous, for surely Gaston Paris has succeeded in demonstrating that *H* is not the original western text; while the majority of Landau's arguments therefore hold also in a comparison of the oldest texts with the Eastern group, it is in view of this fundamental misconception on his part that he has in reality proved nothing more than that the fourteenth century *Historia* is nearer the Hebrew than to any other eastern version.

With the proof of the unoriginality of *H*, the question as to the nearness of the various sub-types of the western group to the parent version has been left open. The oldest text preserved is the *Dolopathos;* but this is a unique version, and, as will be shown in the next chapter, cannot with the slightest probability be looked upon as the western original, though it is assuredly connected in some way with the prevailing type of the Western group, the *Seven Sages of Rome*. Next to the *Dolopathos* the *Scala Coeli* (*S*) and Keller (*K*) texts have been treated as the oldest by the latest and best authorities; to these, in view of its prime importance and the uncertainty as to its relations, we should like to add the type *A**.[1] No proof of the priority of any one of these has yet been brought forward; moreover, the earliest dating proposed for any of them is the first half of the thirteenth century. We may begin, then, with the assumption that the immediate parent version of the Western group has been lost. At the same time, since the *Dolopathos*, which dates from the last quarter of the twelfth century, is evidently based on some version of the prevailing western type, we may assume for

[1] The Old French versions *A, C, D* of Paris (*Deux Rédactions*) have been "starred" throughout in order to avoid confusion with the Middle English (M. E.) versions *A, C, D*.

this lost original a date not later than the middle of the twelfth century.

A twelfth century original having been assumed for the Western group, the *Libro de los Engannos* (XIII cent.), the *Sindibād-nāmeh* (XIV cent.), and the *Seven Vezirs* (very late) may be eliminated from the investigation; likewise the unique text of Nachshebī for reasons that are obvious. There remain the *Mischle Sindbad*, the *Sindban*, and the *Syntipas*, no one of which can be dated later than the eleventh century, if we accept Cassel's view as to the comparative antiquity of the Hebrew text. Further, since the western original of the Western group has been lost, comparison can be made with the latter only on the basis of the constant elements appearing in its most ancient versions,—*S, K, A.** Accordingly, the comparison must be instituted between the Hebrew, Syriac, and Greek versions, on the one hand, and *S, K, A** on the other.

The framework of the romance has undergone a radical change in the course of its transmission westward. There is no longer mention of a philosopher Sindibād, but the seven sages of Rome become the central figures, and play the double rôle of instructors and defenders of the prince. Sundry other characteristic features of the Eastern group, such as the prince's early stupidity, the multiplicity of the king's wives, etc., have been lost; but the most far-reaching change consists in the curtailment of stories, each sage telling only one story in the Western group as against the prevailing number of two in the Eastern.

In these variations the Greek, Hebrew, and Syriac versions present essential agreement; but there are several features in which these three texts do not agree, and it is significant here that where the Western group preserves any of these features, it is always in agreement with the Hebrew, and in no single instance with the Greek or the Syriac.

The following features peculiar to the Hebrew text as compared with the rest of the Eastern group reappear in the oldest western versions:[1]

(1). The seven sages are not referred to simply as such, but are mentioned *by name*[2] (Landau, p. 48).

(2). They vie in their efforts to secure the office of instructor of the prince[3] (Landau, p. 48).

(3). These sages, and not the vezirs or counsellors of the king as with the rest of the Eastern group, relate the stories which preserve the prince's life[4] (Landau, p. 48).

The mode of punishment of the guilty queen offers nothing determining. The eastern texts have little in common here

---

[1] All these several bits of argument adduced here and on the following pages, with the exception of those under the story *avis*, have been advanced by Landau (pp. 47-50); in addition to these, owing to his false hypothesis of the originality of *H*, Landau has made use of two other features in which *H* agrees with the Hebrew text versus the remainder of the Eastern group, but which must be cancelled, since they are also peculiar to *H*. These are (1) the disguised-youth incident of *H*, which Landau (p. 48 f.) inclines to trace back to the seventeenth story of the *Mischle Sindbad*, and (2) *amatores*, the twelfth story of the *Historia*, which is ultimately the same as the Hebrew story of the *Hunchbacks* (*M. S.* 18; see Bédier, *Les Fabliaux*, Paris, 1893, p. 201 f.). Neither of these appears in any other western version, whence the only legitimate inference that they were not in the lost western original, but are late incorporations on the part of *H* into the frame of the collection.

[2] This, a characteristic feature of the Western group, appears in all western texts save those (as *S*) which have been abridged. The names of the sages in the *Mischle Sindbad* are Sindibād, Hippocrates, Apuleius, Lucian, Aristotle, Pindar, and Homer (Cassel, p. 253); in the Western group, Bancillas, Ancilles, Malquidras, Lentulus, Caton, Jesse, and Meros. For variants of these, see Landau, *Quellen des Dekameron*, p. 60 n.

[3] In the Hebrew (see Cassel, p. 255 f.) one proposes to instruct him in five years, another in two years, a third in one year,—and finally Sindibād offers to make him wisest of all men in six months. The term of years proposed by the sages in the western versions varies from seven to one.

[4] Carmoly (p. 65) states expressly that these were the king's counsellors, and not the sages, who, he says, were now in hiding to avoid the king's anger; but, as Landau (p. 48) points out, the sage Aristotle is referred to by name at the end of the third story as having saved the prince's life by his stories on the preceding day (Cassel, p. 267); accordingly, although there is a slight confusion, it is evident that Carmoly is in error.

beyond the bare outline. In the Greek and As-Samarquandī texts, the woman is condemned to wander through the streets on an ass, with her head shaved and her face soiled, and with two criers proclaiming her shame. In the Hebrew text, she is, at the prince's request, pardoned unconditionally. The Syriac text is fragmentary here. Of the western feature of condemning the queen to die the death prepared for the prince, there seems to be no hint in the eastern versions.

A comparison of the four stories (*canis, aper, avis,* and *senescalcus*) common to the two main groups also shows many variations, but here, too, where the *Mischle Sindbad* differs from the *Syntipas* and other versions of the Eastern group, it will be seen to accord in several particulars with the Western group.

(1). *Canis.* The story *canis,* the only one found in all versions of the *Seven Sages,* both eastern and western, exhibits in the earliest western versions no noteworthy variations from the prevailing type of the story in the East. In the *Sindibād-nāmeh* it is a weasel or ichneumon which attacks the sleeping child; in all other versions it is a snake. The child is left in charge of nurses in the western versions, a feature entirely foreign to the Eastern group. The derivative types, *Dolopathos* and *Historia,* introduce a bird (*Dolop.,* a goshawk; *H,* a falcon) which wakes the child on the snake's approach. This and several other additions, especially to the *Dolopathos,* are not found in the types *S, K,* and *A**, a circumstance which well warrants the inference that they were not in the western parent version.

(2). *Aper.* This story, like *canis,* has been subjected to considerable alteration in the course of transmission,—e. g., in the East, the boar comes to his death as the result of holding up his head in the expectation of more fruit (the sinews drying up); in the West, he is slain by the shepherd, who, descending the tree until in reach of him, "claws" him on the back until he falls asleep, and then dispatches him with his knife. But

2

the special value in the collation of this story lies in the fact that the Hebrew text coincides with the Western group in having a *man* chased up the tree, while in the remaining eastern versions it is a *monkey* who thus flees from the boar. This coincidence, first noted by Deslongchamps (*l. c.*, p. 110 n.), is one of the most striking agreements of the Hebrew text with the Western group.

(3). *Senescalcus*. A comparison of the various versions of *senescalcus* reveals no eastern motive reproduced in the West which is not common to the entire Eastern group. The western version of the story agrees in general outline with the eastern, but is distinguished from it by the introduction of even more objectionable details than those which characterize its oriental original. The western texts vary in the method of punishing the seneschal: in *S* he is hanged; in *K*, *A**, and the prevailing sub-groups, he is banished by the king on pain of death in case he return. In the East the bathman (= seneschal) dies by his own hand.

(4). *Avis*. The essential features of this famous story have been preserved remarkably intact thoughout all versions. There are, however, two features which occur in the East only in the *Mischle Sindbad* which have been preserved in the western texts. These are (1) that the wife goes *on the house-top* in order to sprinkle water over the bird's cage, and (2) that she is aided and abetted in her efforts to deceive the bird *by her maid*. Of the first of these we have in no other eastern version any hint; likewise, for the second, there is no real suggestion in any of the Eastern group besides the *Mischle Sindbad*, for, although there is mention elsewhere of the maid, it is only as having been suspected of informing on her mistress, and never in the rôle assigned her in the Hebrew and the western versions.[1]

---

[1] The arguments made by Landau under *avis* are not valid. That the bird speaks Hebrew as well as Latin, is not true of any of the oldest western versions, but appears to be peculiar to *H;* while the argument from the killing of the bird in *H* and the Hebrew text is altogether in-

To recapitulate then, the features peculiar to the Hebrew and the oldest western texts are as follows:

(1). The seven sages are mentioned by name.

(2). There is a rivalry between the sages in their efforts to secure the tutelage of the prince.

(3). The sages, not the king's counsellors, defend the prince.

(4). In *aper*, the adventure happens not to an ape, but to a man.

(5). In *avis*, (a) the deception is practised on the bird through an opening in the house-top, and (b) the maid appears as an assistant of the faithless wife.

A comparison with the *Syntipas* fails to bring out any feature exclusively common to it and the Western group. The same holds for the Syriac and later versions. The question is then narrowed down to the significance of the agreements between the Hebrew and the western texts. Are they only accidental, or have they a real significance? Certainly they do not prove a direct relationship between the Hebrew and any western version, as Deslongchamps and Landau have maintained; nor are they sufficient to justify the thought of a connection of the Eastern and Western groups through intermediate literary stages; indeed, they yield no *conclusive* proof of anything with regard to the problem of relationship. Nevertheless, they are in a measure significant; though *some* of them are in all probability accidental, yet it does not seem possible that all of them can be mere coincidences. They justify, at least, the negative conclusion that neither the *Syntipas* (nor the *Sindban*) was the eastern original whence sprang the tradition which culminated in the parent version of the Western group. And while they do not prove the Hebrew text to represent this eastern original, they do, nevertheless, establish this as a probability, with the only other alternative in the supposition that the eastern original of the Western group has been lost.

valid, since the same feature is found in all eastern versions save the *Syntipas*, and would be in any case of little value for the purpose to which Landau would put it, since it is a simple and natural variation.

I (c). *The Romance in France and Italy.*

Between the eastern and western types of the *Seven Sages*, as has been seen, there is a very wide difference. Four of the original stories and the main outline of the eastern framework have been preserved in the western versions, but, as Comparetti has aptly said, "there is no eastern version which differs so much from the others as the whole Western group differs from the Eastern, whether it be in the form of the fundamental story or in the tales which are inserted in it." In explanation of this wide difference a basis has been assumed for the Western group in oral accounts.

Where these oral accounts first took literary form has not been, and probably never will be, satisfactorily determined. Some have maintained an origin on Latin territory; but the probabilities favor a French origin, though it is more than possible that the parent version was written in the Latin language.

The oldest form, apparently, under which the western type has come down to us is the *Dolopathos*. There can be little doubt, however, that the more widely known *Sept Sages de Rome*, of which there survive many manuscripts dating from a period but a little later than that of the earliest version of the *Dolopathos*, preserves more nearly the form and contents of the western parent version. And it is under this form that the romance has acquired its marvellous popularity in France, whence it has penetrated into nearly every other country of Europe.

With regard to the relationship of these two forms or groups under which the romance appears in the West, early scholars were very much in error. For a long time it was believed that the poetical version of the *Dolopathos* found its source in the Latin prose *Historia Septem Sapientum*;[1] again, it was always assumed as fundamental that the *Historia* antedated

---

[1] The most widely known of all versions of our romance; see below.

and was the ultimate western original of the entire Western group,—these two misconceptions pervaded the entire literature on the romance during the first half of this century. The error of the first was first shown by Montaiglon in 1856,[1] and its utter absurdity was conclusively proved a few years later by Oesterley's discovery of the *Dolopathos* of Johannes, from which Herbert had made his poem.[2] The second was current even until the appearance of Gaston Paris's *Deux Rédactions*[3] in 1876, in which the comparatively recent date of the *Historia*, and its immediate dependence on *A**, has been placed beyond question.

1. The *Dolopathos*.—The *Dolopathos* exists in two versions, the Latin prose of Johannes de Alta Silva and the Old French poem of Herbert. The latter is preserved, so far as is known, in but three manuscripts;[4] of the former, there are known, besides the original manuscript discovered by Oesterley, three late copies pointed out by Mussafia,[5] an Innsbruck,[6] and a British Museum MS.[7]

[1] In the preface to his edition of the Herbert version: *Li Romans de Dolopathos*, ed. Brunet and Montaiglon, Paris, 1856.

[2] This manuscript was discovered by Oesterley in 1873, and was published by him in the same year: *Johannis de Alta Silva Dolopathos* . . . ., Strasburg. See reviews by Paris, *Romania*, II, p. 481 f.; by Studemund, *Z. f. d. A.*, XVII, p. 415 f. and XVIII, p. 221 f.; and by Köhler, *Jahrb. f. rom. u. engl. Lit.*, XIII, p. 328 f. Several manuscripts discovered by Mussafia (*Wiener Akad. Sitzungsb.*, Ph. Hist. Cl., XLVIII, p. 246 f., 1864) prior to this, and at first supposed to be original, were soon shown to be fifteenth century copies of the older manuscript.

[3] Published in the *Soc. d. Anc. Textes fr.* for 1876. For the *Historia*, see pp. XXVIII–XLIII.

[4] See Paris in *Romania*, II, p. 503. A leaf of a fourteenth century MS. of the Herbert version has been lately acquired by the Bibliothèque Nationale —*Nouv. Acq. fr.* 934, No. 6 (*Bulletin de la Soc. d. Anc. Textes fr.*, for 1896, p. 71 f.). See also Haupt's *Altd. Blätter*, I, p. 119 f., for a German version of six stories of the *Dolopathos*.

[5] See *Wiener Akad. Sitzungsb.*, Ph. Hist. Cl., XLVIII, p. 246 f.

[6] Also brought to light by Oesterley.

[7] Usually overlooked; see Ward, *Catalogue of Romances*, London, 1893, II, p. 228 f.

Johannes de Alta Silva, the author of the Latin original, was a Cistercian monk of the monastery of Haute Seille. His work bears the title *Dolopathos, sive Opusculum de rege et septem Sapientibus*. It was dedicated to Bishop Bertrand of Metz, who had jurisdiction over the monastery of Haute Seille from 1184 (when it was transferred from the see of Toul to the see of Metz) to 1212, during which period, since Johannes would naturally dedicate to his own bishop, we may safely place the composition of his work. Paris favors a dating between 1207 and 1212 (*Romania*, II, p. 501).

The Old French poem of Herbert was made from the Latin prose text of Johannes toward the end of the first quarter of the thirteenth century (Montaiglon, 1223-1226 ; Paris, before 1223).

This type of the romance differs from all other western types in having only one instructor for the prince. For this reason it has been conjectured that it was founded on some oriental original, but there is no real evidence in support of this. In the suppression of the queen's stories, a feature in which it agrees with the Nachshebī version, equally as little indication of an immediate eastern original is to be found.

The *Dolopathos* has only one story (*canis*) in common with the Eastern group, and inasmuch as this, together with three other of its stories (*gaza, puteus,* and *inclusa*), is also found in the *Sept Sages de Rome*, it is reasonably certain that the monk Johannes was acquainted with some version of the latter type.[1] There is only one alternative supposition, viz. that both types grew up independently of each other and almost contemporaneously, the one drawing only one story from the traditions brought from the East, while the other drew this and three others in addition,—with the further coincidence that both receive, as the result of like influence and environment, three stories (*gaza, puteus,* and *inclusa*) in common which were not

---

[1] See Comparetti to the contrary; *Vergil in the Middle Ages*, translated by Benecke, London, 1895, p. 234 f.

in the eastern framework. That such was the case is, to say the least, very improbable.

But, in any case, the prose *Dolopathos* was made not from written, but from oral sources. This is expressly stated by its author—who says he wrote *non ut visa, sed ut audita*—and is borne out by the introduction of the *Lohengrin* story, which appears here for the first time,[1] as well as by the variations to which both framework and stories have been subjected.

The poetical version of Herbert is based directly on the Latin prose version of Johannes. It contains many details and several important episodes which do not appear in the text discovered by Oesterley, chief among which additions are (1) the story *inclusa*, which has been fused with *puteus* in the poem, and (2) a very interesting episode with which *gaza* has been supplemented. Gaston Paris[2] thinks that these were contained in Herbert's original, which he believes to have been an enlarged copy of the first draft of the work as seen in the Oesterley manuscript; but whether they are to be thus explained, or are to be attributed to the independence of the poet, has not yet been definitely settled.

The Herbert version is very long, containing nearly 13,000 lines. In both length and style it stands in striking contrast to the Keller metrical version of the *Sept Sages de Rome* (*K*),[3] which, although it has nearly twice as many stories, has only 5,060 lines. The *Dolopathos* has an introduction of about 4,800 lines where *K* has but 68.

The king in this branch of the Western group bears the name Dolopathos, and rules over the island of Sicily. The prince is called Lucinius. Before his birth it is predicted that he will become very wise, but will undergo many hardships, and will ultimately become a worshipper of the true God.

---

[1] See Todd, *La Naissance du Chevalier au Cygne*, Introduction, p. III f., in *Publications of the Mod. Lang. Assn. of America*, vol. IV, 1889. See also Paris's review in *Romania*, XIX, p. 314 f.

[2] *Romania*, II, p. 500.

[3] See the dissertation of Ehret, *Der Verfasser des Roman des Sept Sages und Herbers*, Heidelberg, 1886.

The prince's instruction begins when he has reached the age of seven. He is sent to Rome, and put under the care of the poet Vergil, whose figure is supreme throughout the romance, and gives to it one of its strongest claims upon our interest.[1] The sages, who are, owing to Vergil's prominence, placed somewhat in the background, come up as in the other western versions, one each day and in a most mysterious fashion,— always just in time to save the prince's life. The prince relates no story at all, but Vergil tells the eighth and last. The order of stories is as follows: (1) *canis* (*Dog and Snake*), (2) *gaza* (*King's Treasury*), (3) *senes* (*Best Friend*), (4) *creditor* (the *Pound of Flesh* episode of the *Merchant of Venice*),[2] (5) *viduae filius* (*Widow's Son*), (6) *latronis filius* (*Master-Thief*), (7) *cygni eques* (the fabled origin of Godfrey de Bouillon), (8) *inclusa-puteus* (*Two Dreams* and *Husband Shut Out*).[3]

2. *The Sept Sages de Rome.*—The *Sept Sages de Rome*, in contradistinction to the *Dolopathos*, comprises a very large number of more or less closely related versions. Probably one hundred manuscripts of its type are already known, and many others, we may be sure, remain to be revealed by further research. The immediate source whence these have sprung has not come down to us. The date, too, of the parent version is uncertain, but, in view of its influence on the *Dolopathos* and the comparatively large number of thirteenth century versions, it must be placed as early as 1150, and it may fall in a time considerably anterior to this.

The normal number of stories in this branch is fifteen; of these the queen relates seven, the seven sages one each, and

---

[1] See Comparetti, *Vergil in the Middle Ages*, p. 232 f.

[2] Ward, *Catalogue of Romances*, II, p. 122, makes the slight oversight of asserting that the casket-episode of the *Merchant of Venice* is also introduced into the *Dolopathos*.

[3] These stories have had a wide currency, and, in several instances, a most interesting history. For the fullest collections of analogues to them, see the editions of Montaiglon-Brunet and Oesterley, and the appendix to the latter's edition of the *Gesta Romanorum*.

the prince the fifteenth. The scene of action is prevailingly Rome, though in two instances—*K* and *D*—it is Constantinople.[1] The emperor's name is Diocletian.[2]

The interrelation of the various sub-types into which the *Sept Sages* falls has been the subject of almost continuous investigation for more than half a century. The first serious attempt at an orderly classification was made by Goedeke in 1866 (*Orient und Occident*, III, p. 402 f.). He was followed two years later by Mussafia,[3] in a study which possesses great merit, and which served very much to clear the way for subsequent investigation. But it is to Gaston Paris above all that credit is due here for bringing order out of chaos. The *Préface* to his *Deux Rédactions* is by far the most significant contribution to the study of the *Seven Sages* which has yet been made, and leaves but the one regret that he has not extended his investigations so as to include the problems of the origin and propagation of the romance. It goes without saying that the excellence of Paris's work has been recognized on all sides, and that his conclusions have been almost universally adopted.

Paris classifies in five sub-groups, as follows:

1. *S*. The *Scala Coeli* abridgment published by Goedeke.
2. *K*. The well known metrical version of Keller.
3. *H*. The very large group, of which the *Historia* is the type.
4. *I*. The *Versio Italica*.
5. French prose versions (other than *H*), including *A**, *L*, *D** (*V*), and *M*.

1. *S*. The first of these, the text contained in the *Scala Coeli*, a compilation of the early fourteenth century by the Dominican Johannes Junior, is a Latin prose abridgment of a lost *Liber de Septem Sapientibus*. For the latter, Goedeke

---

[1] This is only partly true of *D*; see Paris, *Deux Rédactions*, p. 1.

[2] There are several exceptions to this: in *K* he is called Vespasian; in *D**, Marcomeris, son of Priam (!); in *H*, Pontianus,—the name Diocletian being transferred to the prince.

[3] *Wiener Akad. Sitzungsb.*, Ph. Hist. Cl., LVII, p. 37 f.

(who has published the text according to the *Scala Coeli* in *Orient u. Occident*, III, p. 402 f.) conjectures a date in the first half of the thirteenth century. An extract in the *Summa Recreatorum* (XV cent.), which agrees very closely with *S*, has been pointed out by Mussafia (*Wiener Akad. Sitzungsb.*, Ph. Hist. Cl., LVII, p. 83 f.).

S differs materially from *H*, and is almost as far from *K* and D^*. It stands nearest to *L*, having in common with it the two stories *filia* and *noverca* in the place of *Roma* and *inclusa* of the remaining types. The agreement with D^*, in that the queen is defended on the last day by a champion, is doubtless a mere coincidence (Paris, *l. c.*, p. VIII). Its only influence seems to have been that exercised on *L*. For Goedeke's claim that it is the closest extant representative of the western original no sustaining argument has yet been brought forward.[1]

2. *H*. The type of the second group is the well-known *Historia Septem Sapientum Romae*. Buchner[2] enumerates sixteen manuscripts in which the *Historia* has been preserved. Its first edition appeared at Cologne in 1472, and the bibliographers report many of subsequent date. The latest edition, and only nineteenth century reprint, is that of Buchner.[3] An Old French translation, printed at Geneva in 1492, has recently been republished by Paris as the second text of his *Deux Rédactions* (pp. 55–205). The *Historia Calumnia Novercali* (Antwerp, 1496) differs from it mainly in the omission of all Christian features.

The *Historia* is by far the most widely known of all western versions, having had equally as great a vogue in some other European countries—Germany for instance—as in France. In English the Wynkyn de Worde text (to which

---

[1] Ward, *Catalogue of Romances*, II, p. 200, erroneously states that Paris upholds Goedeke here.

[2] *Erlanger Beiträge zur englischen Philologie*, V, p. 1. Of these six were first pointed out by Paris, *l. c.*, p. XXXIX,—eight by Varnhagen, *Eine Ital. Prosaversion d. Sieben Weisen*, p. XV.

[3] *Erlang. Beitr.*, V, pp. 7–90. An Innsbruck MS. which dates from 1342.

the many English chap-book versions owe their origin), the Copland, and the Rolland versions found in it their ultimate original. With the Germans the *Historia* type is practically the only one which has found acceptance, and the number of versions, either in Latin or German, which are contained in their libraries is very large.[1] It is under this form, also, that the romance has acquired its popularity in other Germanic and in the Slavonic languages.[2]

The history of opinion with regard to this type of the romance possesses much interest. Until quite recently, as has been seen, *H* was supposed to be the oldest member of the Western group. Goedeke, in 1866, was the first to break with this tradition, but without showing why. Paulin Paris followed in 1869, throwing the question open.[3] Comparetti, also, in the same year, expressed the opinion that *H* was far from representing the western original.[4] The matter was not satisfactorily cleared up until the appearance of Gaston Paris's book in 1876. The results of Paris's investigation (*l. c.*, p. XXVIII f.) are to entirely dethrone *H* from the position which had been traditionally accorded it, and to establish for it a date in the first half of the fourteenth century, and an immediate basis on type *A**.[5]

The distinguishing features of *H*, aside from its slight difference from *A** in the order of stories, are the introduction

---

[1] For the first general discussion of the romance in Germany, see the preface to Keller's *Li Romans des Sept Sages*, Tübingen, 1837. A more comprehensive discussion of the German versions accompanies his edition of the Hans von Bühel metrical version, *Diocletianus Leben* (Quedlinburg, 1841).

[2] Keller enumerates versions, either in manuscript or in print, in Dutch, Welsh, Icelandic, Swedish, Danish, Polish, Hungarian, Russian, and Armenian; see the prefaces to his two editions cited above. See, also, Murko, "Die Geschichte v. d. Sieben Weisen b. d. Slaven" in *Wiener Akad. Sitzungsb.*, Ph. Hist. Cl., CXXII, 1890, and "Beitr. zur Textgesch. d. H. S. S." in *Zeitschr. f. vergl. Lit.-gesch.*, pp. 1-34, 1892.

[3] *Biblioph. Français*, IV, p. 69 f.   [4] *Book of Sindibâd*, p. 47.

[5] It is hard to see how Landau, *Quellen des Dekameron*, 2d ed., p. 51 f., and a few others, can still persist in their adherence to the old view.

of the stories *amatores* and *amici* (the latter appended to *vaticinium*), the fusion of *senescalcus* and *Roma*, and its unusual mass of details.

3. *K.* The Old French metrical version, *Li Romans des Sept Sages*, was published by Keller, at Tübingen, in 1836. Of this version there exists only one complete manuscript, to which its editor gives a date in the late thirteenth century. A fragment of a metrical text agreeing closely with it in content, but differing slightly in order of stories, is preserved in MS. 620 of the Library of Chartres.[1] An edition of this has been promised by Paris.

K has the same stories as *D** and *A**, but in a different order. The agreement in order, as also in incident, is, as a rule, closest with *D**; in the stories *vidua, Roma, inclusa,* and *vaticinium,* however, *K* exhibits a very close, at times even verbal, agreement with *A**. In explanation of this, the possibility of an influence of *K* on *A** is precluded by the fact that the former is of earlier date; hence it is necessary to posit for *A** and *K* a common source, designated by Paris as *V*.

4. *I.* The *Versio Italica* was first so styled by Mussafia in his study of the Italian versions, in *Jahrb. f. rom. u. englische Lit.*, IV, p. 166 f., 1862. This group consists of six versions, three of which are in Latin. One of the latter has been brought to light only within the last few years;[2] one was published by Mussafia (*Wiener Akad. Sitzungsb.*, Ph. Hist. Cl., LVII, p. 94 f.) in 1868, and is well known; and the third is the British Museum MS. Addl. 15685.[3] Of the Italian versions one is in verse,[4] but of late date,—Rajna in his description (*Romania*, VII, pp. 22 f., 369 f.; X, p. 1 f.) plac-

---

[1] See Paris, *l. c.*, p. III n., and Paul Meyer in the *Bulletin d. l. Soc. des Anc. Textes français*, 1894, p. 40 f. The order of stories here is—*tentamina, Roma, avis, sapientes, vidua, Virgilius, inclusa, vaticinium*. For the order in *K* and other versions, see the comparative table, p. 35.

[2] By Murko; see *Romania*, XX, p. 373.

[3] Ward, *Catalogue of Romances*, II, p. 207 f. Hitherto unnoticed in this connection.

[4] Edited by Rajna, *Storia di Stefano*, Bologna, 1881.

ing it between 1440 and 1480. The two remaining Italian versions early underwent publication, one in 1832 by Della Lucia,[1] the other by Cappelli in 1865.[2]

The order of stories in *I* is materially different from that in any other group or version. The queen in this group, instead of relating the first story, follows in each instance the sage, thus reversing the order,—2 becoming 1, 4–3, and so on. In consequence of this innovation, the number of stories is reduced to fourteen, the seventh being crowded out.[3]

In the absence of the *filia-noverca* and *amatores-amici* features, *I* groups itself with *K*, *D**, and *A**. Its closest agreement in incident is with *A**, in which recent scholars believe it to have had its source.[4]

The modern Italian *Erasto*, which at one time was placed by itself as representing a free adaptation of the romance, and as bearing a somewhat similar relation to the remaining Italian versions as the *Dolopathos* to the prevailing French type, is now universally acknowledged to be an offspring of the *Versio Italica*. The *Erasto* has been very popular in its own country, and has been translated into other languages. The first edition of it appeared at Venice in 1542, the last in 1841. An English translation was made by Frances Kirkman in 1674.

5. French Prose Redactions. The number of French prose redactions is very large. Paris already in 1876 knew of nineteen manuscripts in Paris, besides the four in Brussels, and one in the Cambridge University Library. A number of others have been since pointed out.[5]

[1] Della Lucia, *Novella antica scritta nel buon sec. d. lingua*, Venice, 1832.
[2] Cappelli, *Il libro dei sette savi di Roma*, Bologna, 1865.
[3] It is interesting to note here that the story thus discarded is *senescalcus*,— a feature in which the *Versio Italica* has anticipated one of the English versions—Cambridge Ff, II, 38 (*F*).
[4] See, for the most recent opinion, Rajna in *Romania*, VII, p. 369 f.
[5] These are mentioned under the discussion of the various groups into which they fall.

(1). Paris classifies under the sub-groups *D** (*V*), *L*, *A**, and *M*. Of these *M*—the *Male Marastre*—is of little interest other than as showing the immense popularity of the romance in the thirteenth century. Only three manuscripts of it have so far been brought to light. In all these the emperor is Diocletian and the prince, Fiseus; Marcus, son of Cato, is given prominence; and, a feature which distinguishes this sharply from all other groups, *six new stories* are substituted for a corresponding number of those in the prevailing types. The original of *M* is believed to have been made on a very mutilated manuscript of the *A**-type. The new stories, which are of a much lower order than those they displace, are probably the invention of the author.[1]

(2). With *M* may be associated the numerous 'continuations'[2] of the *Sept Sages* in French, of which the most important is the *Marques de Rome*. This type originated in Picardy in the thirteenth century. A version of it has been recently published by Alton (*Li Romans de Marques de Rome*, Tübingen, 1889). In the introduction to this edition, the editor states that the romance was certainly not written later than 1277, and probably even forty years earlier (Alton, p. XIV). It seems to have met with considerable popularity, as Alton describes ten manuscripts which still survive. It doubtless had its ultimate basis in *A**—Alton thinks with *M* as an intervening stage, but Paris (*Romania*, XIX, p. 493) denies this, maintaining that *M* is posterior to the *Marques*.

(3). *D**. The *Version Dérimée*, a unique prose manuscript published by Paris as the first text of his *Deux Rédactions* (pp. 1–55), is thus called on account of the numerous instances of rime still discernible in the text, and which prove beyond doubt a metrical original.[3]

---

[1] See Paris, *l. c.*, p. XXIII f.

[2] For these compare P. Paris, *Les MSS. français de la Bibl. du Roi*, Paris, 1836, I, p. 109 f. More accessible in Leroux de Lincy, *l. c.*, p. x f.

[3] This was first shown by Paris, *Deux Rédactions*, p. v f.

D^* agrees more closely with K than with any other known version. It cannot have been based on K, however, as Paris has shown, but the two doubtless flow from a common source, which Paris designates as V. From this V, also, the Chartres manuscript was in all probability made (Paris, *l. c.*, p. x.)

(4). There remain the two families L and A^*. The first of these comprises all versions of the type of the first Leroux de Lincy print,[1] in which the order of stories is *arbor, canis, aper, medicus, gaza, puteus, senescalcus, tentamina, Virgilius, avis, sapientes, noverca, filia.* Only six manuscripts (four strictly according to L, and two slightly influenced by A^*) were known to Paris (*l. c.*, p. 10 f.). To these must be added the Catalan version in *ottava rima*, edited by Mussafia (*Wiener Akad. Denkschr.*, xxv, p. 185 f., 1876), and five Old French prose manuscripts, partly fragmentary, enumerated by Paul Meyer in *Bulletin de la Soc. des Anc. Textes fr.* for 1894, p. 38 f.[2]

In its employment of the stories *filia* and *noverca*, L at once groups itself with S. This, however, is not the only feature which the two types have in common. A general comparison with the rest of the Western group serves to show that (if we may except A^* for the time being) S is also nearest to L in motive (Paris, *l. c.*, p. XII). In order of stories, too, S and L fall together, the only differences being the reversal on the part of L of *tentamina* and *puteus*, and the suppression of *vidua* and *vaticinium*. Paris has therefore concluded that L was made on a manuscript of S which was mutilated toward the end, and that the scribe has in consequence had to trust to his memory for his last stories (*l. c.*, p. XIII).

[1] Leroux de Lincy, *Romans des Sept Sages*, Paris, 1838, pp. 1-76.

[2] Meyer does not express himself definitely as to the class of but one of these—the Chartres MS., which he groups with L. He implies, however, in his statement that the Bib. Nat. fragment (p. 39, n. 2) belongs to A^*, that all the rest belong to L. Nevertheless, his notices leave the impression that some of these manuscripts (possibly all except the two just mentioned) have not been handled, and that a part of them may yet be found to belong to the larger group A^*.

(5). *A**, the largest and most important of all French groups, has been reserved for the last place. To this family pertain, besides its immediate members, the groups *Marques*, *M*, *I*, and *H;* it is, then, the original, either directly or indirectly, of four-fifths of the manuscripts and prints of the romance which survive. It is not only the ultimate source of all Italian versions,—whether direct, as with the D'Ancona edition, or indirect through *I*, but it is also, through *H*, the parent of almost all the manifold versions of the *Sept Sages* outside of Romance. And, what is of prime interest and importance to the English student, it was some manuscript of this group which furnished the immediate original of the Middle English versions.

Under group *A** Paris includes all manuscripts of the type of the Italian version published by D'Ancona.[1] He enumerates in his preface (p. XVI f.), in addition to the Italian version whence the group is named, fourteen manuscripts in Old French,[2] several of which date from the thirteenth century. Four other manuscripts, pointed out since the appearance of Paris's work (Brit. Mus. Harl. 3860 [XIV cent.], St. Jno. Bapt. Coll., Oxf., 102 [XIV cent.],[3] Cambr. Univy. Liby. Gg. 6, 28,[4] and a fragment in the Bib. Nat.-Nouv. Acq. fr. 1263 [XIII cent.]),[5] increase the number of French versions to eighteen. To this family, also, belongs the British Museum Italian prose version published by Varnhagen.[6]

The text of *A**[7] falls into two parts,—the first eleven stories (A_1*) being textually very close to *L*, while the last four (A_2*), as Paris has shown, agree very closely with *K*.

---

[1] *Il Libro dei Sette Savj di Roma*, Pisa, 1864.

[2] One of these is the manuscript 2137 of the Bib. Nat., published in part by Leroux de Lincy, pp. 79–110.

[3] For these two, cf. Varnhagen, *Z. f. rom. Ph.*, I, p. 555 f. See also for the first, Ward, *l. c.*, II, p. 199 f.

[4] *Romania*, XV, p. 348.

[5] Delisle, *MSS. lat. et fr. ajoutées aux Fondes*, etc., Paris, 1891, I, p. 259.

[6] *Eine Ital. Prosaversion der Sieben Weisen*, Berlin, 1881.

[7] By this is meant the second Leroux de Lincy redaction. Other versions of this type, as, *e. g.*, MS. 6849 (new No. 189), are not so close to *L*.

The composite nature of the text Paris explains as due to the fact that the scribe primarily employed a fragment of L containing only eleven tales, and that K, or its source, V, has been used for the remaining four tales.[1] And this seems to be borne out by internal evidence; for A_2* not only falls in with K as regards incident, but, as in the case of D*, there is often even a textual agreement in which entire lines that appear in K are reproduced.[2] Yet, as already observed, this metrical original of A_2* cannot have been K, since there are a number of A*-manuscripts which antedate the latter, especially if we may accept Keller, who despite his maintenance of the priority of K, ventured a date no earlier than 1284, or later in all probability than the composition of the English parent text. Moreover, a comparison of A_2* with K and D* will show that each of the latter possesses features in common with A* which are not found in the other. The original of A_2* must therefore be sought in some other version than K,—probably, as Paris assumes, in V.[3]

[1] *Deux Rédactions*, p. xviii.
[2] *Ibid.*, p. xix, for a citation of parallel passages from A_2* and K. Almost as noteworthy agreement will be found in some of the remaining stories.
[3] But can this be final? Is it not possible, however improbable it may seem, that the manuscripts of A* which have survived were ultimately based on a metrical text which preserved the A*-order of stories (or, at least, was nearer the A*-order than the K-, C*- or D*-order), and which was closely related with V? In this case, of course, L (the first eleven stories), would have to be explained as based on A* (rather than the reverse, as with Paris), and A_2* as representing a prosing of a portion of the metrical A*, to which K has very nearly approached. Against this view would be the strong evidence submitted by Paris. In favor of it, however, are the considerations (1) that this would better account for the popularity of the A*-type during the first half of the thirteenth century; (2) that the Middle English versions both favor a metrical original and were based on a text nearer to K in many details than is the De Lincy print of A*; (3) that to base A* on L, and consequently, as Paris maintains, ultimately on S, is to connect it with a different line of tradition from that which it seems to follow (cf. certain textual agreements with K which A*, L exhibit: p. 16: "comme il fist au cheualier de son leureier" = K 1141-2: "Comme il fist au cheualier, Ki atort occist son leurier;" p. 39: "Il apela son seneschal" = K 1509: "Lors apiela son seneschal;" p. 40: "Vos gerrez auec le

Resumé. Looked at externally the Western group falls into two main sub-groups, the *Dolopathos* and the *Sept Sages de Rome*. The *Dolopathos*, however, did not develop from the Eastern group independently, but must have had an ultimate basis (doubtless through an oral medium) on some version of the larger group.

The *Sept Sages de Rome*, as regards order and content of stories, also falls into two groups,—one represented by S and L, the other by K, D^*, C^*, (V), and A^* and its variants, I, H, M, and *Marques*. Peculiar to the former group (S, L) are the stories *filia* and *noverca*, to the latter the stories *Roma* and *inclusa*.

Which of these groups represents most faithfully the lost western original is, at the present stage of our knowledge, impossible to determine, but the fact that the *Dolopathos* of Herbert contains the story *inclusa* seems to point to the priority of the K-, D^*-, A^*-group.[1]

With respect to the separate sub-groups, L may have been based on A^* and S, though the view of Paris, that it had its basis in S alone, carries with it greater probability. Either explanation leaves the origin of S unexplained. K, D^*, C^* go back to the same lost metrical original, V. A^* is probably to be explained with Paris as having its source in L and V, though this, as yet, has been by no means established. It is not improbable that a metrical version of A^* existed at some time.

roi"$= K$ 1531: "Auoeques le roi vous girois;" p. 50: "Qui me ferra, je trerai jà"$= K$ 3938: "Ki me ferra, je trairai ia"); (4) that we may still find in A^*, what appear to be reflections of a versified original; thus, p. 15: "Celz que je mout amoie et en qui je me fioie;" p. 23: "Li sangliers vint vers l'alier, si commença à mengier," and "quant il vit le sanglier, si s'en volt aler;" p. 33: "Quant eles virent lor père trainer, si commencièrent (à brère et) à crier;" p. 50: "Sire, il ot en ceste vile un clerc qui ot non Vergile." When all this is said, however, the case is by no means strong, and we would not presume to insist on this theory as presenting the probability, by any means, which attaches to the view set forth by Paris; it is merely suggested as an alternate possibility, which has not yet been disposed of.

[1] See also, Paris, *Romania*, IV, p. 128, for the additional evidence in support of this view drawn from the story *Roma*.

Table of Stories in the Western Versions.[1]

A*	L	S	K	D*	H	I	M	Dolopathos.
arbor	arbor	arbor	arbor	arbor	arbor	——	arbor	——
canis	canis	canis	canis	canis	canis	canis	canis	canis
aper	aper	aper	senesc.	senesc.	aper	arbor	aper	——
medicus	medicus	medicus	medicus	medicus	puteus	medicus	medicus	gaza
gaza	gaza	gaza	aper	aper	gaza	aper	gaza	——
puteus	puteus	tentam.	puteus	puteus	avis	tentam.	avis	senes
senescalcus	senesc.	senesc.	sapient.	sapient.	sapient.	sapient.	filius	——
tentamina	tentam.	puteus	tentam.	tentam.	tentam.	avis	vidua	creditor
Virgilius	Virgil.	Virgil.	Roma.	Roma.	Virgil.	gaza	nutrix	——
avis	avis.	avis.	avis	avis	medicus	inclusa	Antenor	vid.—fil.
sapientes	sapient.	sapient.	gaza	gaza	sen.—Rom.	Roma	spurius	——
vidua	noverca	vidua	vidua	vidua	amatores	vidua	cardamum	latro.—fil.
Roma	filia	filia	Virgil.	Virgil.	inclusa	Virgil.	assass.	——
inclusa	——	noverca	inclusa	inclusa	vidua	puteus	inclusa	cyg.—eq.
vaticinium	——	vaticin.	vaticin.	vatic. +	vat.—amici.	vaticin.	vaticin.	incl.—put.

II. THE ROMANCE IN ENGLAND.

The enormous popularity of the *Seven Sages* in French found but a faint reflection in early English. So far, only eight Middle English versions have been brought to light, and as at least seven of these go back to the same lost original, it appears that the romance did not at first take a very firm root in English soil. Nor has it in more recent times acquired the popularity in England that it enjoyed in other countries of Europe; for, besides the numerous chap-book versions, all which are of a low order of excellence, there have survived only two versions belonging to the Modern English period.

Yet, despite this comparatively small popularity of the romance in England, it is very evident that the English

---

[1] The order of the fragmentary Old French metrical version *C** is as follows:—*tentamina, Roma, avis, sapientes, vidua, Virgilius, inclusa, vaticinium.* In the Varnhagen Italian prose version, *puteus* has been supplanted by a new story, which V. calls *mercator*. All the Middle English versions save *F* (for which see p. 62 of this study) follow the *A**-order. The later English versions belong to group *H*.

versions have not received attention commensurate with their importance. Indeed, there is no department of the study of the *Seven Sages*, much neglected though all have unfortunately been, which has been more neglected than the English. Weber, the first in the field, offered with his edition of the Auchinleck text practically no introduction at all.[1] Likewise Wright, in the essay which accompanied the Cambridge text (Dd, I, 17), while he presented an abstract of the *Historia*, confined the discussion of his own text, singularly enough, to less than two pages.[2] Besides these, Ellis in his *Specimens*,[3] Clouston in his *Book of Sindibād*,[4] and Gomme in the preface to his reprint of the Wynkyn de Worde edition[5] have submitted analyses of the Weber, Wright, and Wynkyn de Worde editions respectively, and sundry others have made incidental references; but there has so far appeared only one detailed and serious investigation of the problems which the English versions present—the dissertation *Ueber die mittelenglischen Fassungen der Sage von den sieben weisen Meistern*, Breslau, 1885, by Paul Petras. This scholar, in dealing with the source and inter-connection of the English versions, has arrived at some very gratifying results, but his work leaves much to be desired. Three of the eight Middle English versions have escaped notice at his hands, as also, for some unaccountable reason, the well-known edition of Wynkyn de Worde,—and a good half of his conclusions may be overthrown by a more thorough investigation. In view, then, of this manifest neglect of the English versions another detailed study of them—especially of the relations of the Middle

[1] *Metrical Romances*, Edinburgh, 1810, I, p. LV and III, pp. 1-153.
[2] *The Seven Sages*, Percy Society Publications, vol. XVI, p. LXVIII, London, 1845; also in Warton's *History of English Poetry*, ed. Hazlitt, London, 1871, I, p. 305 f.
[3] *Specimens of Early English Metrical Romances*, London, 1811, III, pp. 1-101.
[4] *Book of Sindibād* [Glasgow], 1884, p. 327 f.
[5] *The History of the Seven Wise Masters of Rome*, published for the Villon Society, London, 1885.

English manuscripts—will not, it is believed, be deemed untimely.

II (a). *The Middle English Versions.*

The Middle English group comprises eight known versions, in as many different manuscripts. All these are in verse, and in the octosyllabic or four-stressed couplet. They are as follows: Auchinleck (*A*), Arundel 140 (*Ar*), Egerton 1995 (*E*), Balliol College 354 (*B*), Cambridge Ff, II, 38 (*F*), Cotton Galba E, IX (*C*), Cambridge Dd, I, 17 (*D*), and Asloan (*As*).[1]

1. *Description of the Manuscripts.*

A.—The Auchinleck MS. of the Advocate's Library, Edinburgh, denoted throughout as *A*. For a general description of this manuscript, see Kölbing, *Englische Studien*, VII, p. 185 f. The text of the *Seven Sages* occupies ff. 85a–99d, and is fragmentary at both beginning and end, only 2645 lines remaining. It has been published by Weber, *Metrical Romances*, Edinburgh, 1810, III, pp. 1–153, where it comprises lines 135–2779, the Cotton MS. (*C*) having been used for the remainder. For a collation of this edition with the manuscript, see Kölbing, *Englische Studien*, VI, p. 443 f. Copious extracts with an analysis may be found in Ellis's *Specimens*, London, 1811, III, pp. 1–101. With regard to date of composition there is no internal evidence other than linguistic; since, however, the Auchinleck MS. dates from about 1330, the composition of *A* must fall before that time.[2] The form

---

[1] I have handled and made transcripts of all these manuscripts save those which have been printed and the Asloan. Five of them (*A, E, C, F,* and *D*) have been studied either in whole or in part by Petras, and the Asloan MS. was also known to him through Laing's very incomplete description of it in the preface to his edition of the Rolland text, p. XII. Of the Arundel and Balliol manuscripts Petras was apparently unaware.

[2] Cf. Morsbach, *M. E. Grammatik*, Halle, 1896, p. XI, and Brandl in *Paul's Grundriss*, II, 1, p. 635.

hardly justifies a dating earlier than 1300. In text and metre *A* is, as a rule, very good, though in both there are occasional imperfections and corruptions.¹ The dialect is Kentish, though not of the strict type.²

Ar.—MS. Arundel 140 of the British Museum,—cited as *Ar*. Paper, dating from the first half of the fifteenth century. For general description, see Ward, *Catalogue of Romances*, II, p. 224. This text occupies ff. 152–165b, and is fragmentary, beginning with the conclusion of *aper* (3) and ending with the 21st line of *vaticinium* (15); 2565 lines remain. It is very much faded, and in many cases illegible, especially at the end of the b- and at the beginning of the c-columns. With regard to initial capitalization, it is very irregular. A line has been lost after l. 618; after l. 919 an extra line has been introduced with no corresponding rime. The text is metrically very poor, and many final *e*'s have to be inserted in order to secure the required four stresses; there are also a number of imperfect rimes (such as *yspede : saue*, 243–4) and other textual irregularities; nevertheless, *Ar*, as is shown below, is the closest representative of the lost M. E. original. The dialect is Kentish.³ The text has not been published.

¹ There are many emendations which lie on the surface and which are sustained by the closely related versions *Ar*, *E*, etc. Some of these are: (1) for *schild* 1016 read *schuld(e)*—cf. *F* 1487, *Ar*, *B*, *E*; (2) for *swich* 1031 read *syke* or *seke*—cf. *Ar* 91, etc.; (3) for *tol of* 2050 read *to lof*—cf. *E* 2082, etc.; (4) for *to-delue* 2417 read *go delue*—cf. *B* 2509, etc.; (5) after *He* 2657, insert þouȝt—cf. *Ar* 1782, etc.

² A. S. *y* is regularly represented by the *e*-sound, though this may not always be graphic. Of the 27 determining rimes, 22, or 81 per cent., have the *e*-coloring. There is nothing in other developments to contradict this result. The only Northern forms in the rime are a pres. part. in -*and*, 1977–8, and two instances of the third pers. sing. of the present tense in *s*, 615–6 and 937–8.

³ To the development of A. S. *y* (stable or unstable, long or short) into *e*, there is only one certain exception: *wyne : syne*, 691–2. Elsewhere we find only the *e*-quality; cf. *nede : hyde*, 383–4; *ifet : iknet*, 601–2; *gardyner : fyr*, 863–4, 872–3; also 892–3, 939–40, 979–80, 1433–4, 1515–6, 1535–6, 1541–2, 1583–4, 1761–2, 1847–8, 2059–60. The additional rime-evidence is altogether confirmatory of a Southern scribe: A. S. $\bar{a} > \bar{o}$ unexceptionally, the

E.—MS. Egerton 1995 of the British Museum,[1]—cited throughout as *E*. Ff. 3–54b. Paper, dating from the fifteenth century,—probably the second half.[2] Written in single columns, with initials in red. Very regular as regards capitalization. Complete, containing 3588 lines, and bearing the title *Seven Sages of Rome*, with the colophon *Expliciunt Septem Sapientes*. Before the first story, *arbor*, stands the simple rubric, "He[re] begynnythe the fyrste tale of the Emperasse;" before nine others, there is substituted for this a couplet indicating the contents of the story which follows, as *e. g.*, *canis* (695–6):

'Here begynnythe the tale of a knyght
That cylde hys grehounde with unryght.'

The stories *avis*, *vidua*, *Roma*, *inclusa*, and *vaticinium* have nothing corresponding to this. The dialect is Kentish, though less strongly marked than in *Ar*.[3] No edition of *E* has yet appeared. An extract, including ll. 2251–2358, accompanies the monograph of Petras, "Anhang," p. 54 f.

B.—MS. No. 354 of Balliol College Library, Oxford,— denoted as *B*.[4] Ff. 18a–54b. Paper, belonging to the early pres. part. (except *buland : blynd*, 1589–90) ends in -*ng*, the verb is Southern (save *cryén: mene*, 2556–7, where we have a Midland form), the past part. preserves, as a rule, the prefix, and rejects (in the case of the strong verb) the ending, etc. Within the line, however, there are occasional Northern forms, particularly of the pres. part., as *buland*, 1588, 1591, 1599, *brynand*, 1922; but these are by no means the rule, the Southern form being in general preserved as well within the line as in the rime.

[1] For a general description of this manuscript, see Ward's *Catalogue*, II, p. 218 f.
[2] See the sixth article: "Gregory Skinner's Chronicle of the Mayors of London, ending in 1469," ff. 113–122b.
[3] The usual development of A. S. *y* is *e*, or the *e*-quality,—see the rimes of ll. 245–6, 577–8, 783–4, 845–6, 1323–4, 1545–6, 1799–1800, 1821–1822; but occasionally *y*,—cf. *kynne: lynne* (O.N. *linna*), 1317–8 and *wynne: syne*, 1635–6. The evidence is otherwise strongly indicative of a Southern scribe, though a few Northern forms are borne out by the rime; cf. *hondys: stondys* (3d sing.), 439–40, also *kynge: yonge*, 93–4, and *yonge: connynge*, 3581–2.
[4] The existence of this version of the *Seven Sages* was first pointed out by Varnhagen, in his *Eine Ital. Prosav. d. Sieben Weisen*, Berlin, 1881, p. XI; see in the same connection his review of Petras, *Eng. Stud.*, X, p. 279 f.

sixteenth century.[1] In single columns; irregular in capitalization. Described in Coxe's *Catalogus*, I, p. 110, as in the hand of John Hyde. The text is complete, containing 3708 lines. The first rubric, which contains the title, reads as follows: "Here begynneth þe prologes of the VII. sagis or VII. wise masters which were named as here-after ffollowing." Each story has a heading or title, as *e. g.*, *arbor:* "The empresse tale off the pynote tree." At the end of the text stands the colophon: "Thus endith of the VII. sages of Rome, which was drawen owt of crownycles *and* owt of wrytyng of old men, *and* many a notable tale is ther-in, as ys beffore sayde. Quod Richard Hill." This manuscript contains very few abbreviations, and the language is much modernized. In line 1761: "On the ffall suche as fell to a old man by his wif," we have two lines in one. The rime is, if anything, slightly better than in *A, Ar,* and *E,* but is, nevertheless, occasionally imperfect, cf. *visage: noyse,* 459–60; assonance, as in all other related M. E. texts, abounds; often four lines rime together, and occasionally six, cf. 2583–8. The dialect is Southern.[2] No edition of the text has yet appeared, but the E. E. T. S. has for some time been advertising the entire manuscript as needing editing.

F.—MS. Ff, II, 38 (formerly marked *More 690*) of the Cambridge University Library,—denoted as *F*.[3] Ff. 134a–156d. Paper, dating from about the middle of the fifteenth century. Written in double columns of about 40 ll. to the column. Handwriting uniform; irregular as to capitalization, though most lines begin with a capital. The beginnings of stories indicated merely by large initial capitals in red.

---

[1] Cf. Art. 31, "Memoranda of Richard Hill," and Art. 98, "Names of Mayors (of London)."

[2] Southern forms are sustained by the rime almost without exception. A. S. *y* is represented by both *y* and *e*, in about equal proportion; the rimes in *e* are probably to be explained, however, as reminiscences of a Kentish original.

[3] Cf. Halliwell, *Thornton Romances*, Camden Society, vol. XXX, p. XXXVI f., and the Cambridge Univ. Lib. *Catalogue of MSS.*, II, p. 408.

The text is fragmentary; ff. 141 and 144 (or less than 400
ll.) have been lost, and fol. 135 is in a mutilated condition;[1]
2555 ll. remain. Criteria for determining the dialect are not
abundant, as the manuscript is late and the forms are somewhat mixed; but the bulk of the evidence favors a Southern
dialect.[2] The text has not been edited, although, in view
of its uniqueness, it is not uninteresting, and in its last four
stories is of considerable value. Extracts are given by Halliwell, *Thornton Romances*, p. XLIII f., Wright, *The Seven Sages*,
p. LXX f., and Petras, *l. c.*, p. 60 f.

C.—MS. Cotton Galba E, IX, of the British Museum,—
denoted as C.[3] Ff. 25b–48b. Vellum; in double columns, with
initials in blue and red, and in a very plain hand of the first
third of the fifteenth century. Complete, in 4328 ll. Bearing
the title þe *Proces of þe Seuyn Sages*. Each prolog and each
story marked off by rubrics: in the case of the former, such
as " Here bigins þe fyrst proces " (called " prolong " after the
fourth story), with the latter, " Here bygins þe first tale of
þe whyfe," etc., the number being given in each instance,
and, in the case of the masters' stories, their names also.
The dialect is Northern. Both text and metre are very
pure;[4] the rime, especially, stands in marked contrast to the
Southern versions, being almost free of assonance and the im-

---

[1] The Cambridge *Catalogue* fails to specify the leaves which have been lost.
Petras (p. 8) and others go to the other extreme in asserting that the text
is very incomplete.

[2] A. S. $\bar{a} > \bar{o}$, and the forms of the verb, with the exception of the strong
past part., where -*en* is the usual ending, are Southern. The scribe, however, probably belonged rather to the middle or western South than to
Kent, or its neighborhood; cf. the rimes in *y* where the *ü*-quality prevails:
tyme: kynne, 813–4; *wytte: pytte*, 845–6; *hym: kynne*, 871–2; 1348–9, 1636–7,
etc. The rimes *bedd: hydd*, 200–1, and *kende: sende*, 1890–1, are probably
to be traced to the Kentish original.

[3] Cf. Ward's *Catalogue*, II, p. 213 f., for a general description of this manuscript.

[4] There are very few verses that are too short (among these are 84, 443,
911, 1868, 1901, 1918, 2973), and almost none that are too full (cf. 843).
Among the few inexact rimes are *sages: message*, 355–6; *brend: assent*, 2321–
2; *hew: mowe*, 2842–3.

perfections in which the latter abound. No complete edition of *C* has so far appeared; but lines 1–134 and 3108–4328 are printed in Weber, *Metr. Rom.*, III, pp. 1 f. and 108 f., where this text has been employed to supplement *A*. The story *avis*, comprising lines 2411–2548, appears in the "Anhang" to Petras's monograph, p. 56 f.[1]

D.—MS. Dd, I, 17 of the Cambridge University Library,—cited as *D*.[2] Ff. 54a, col. 1—63a, col. 3. Parchment; in treble columns; appears to belong to the end of the fourteenth century.[3] Textually very imperfect, and plainly the work of a careless scribe. Thirteen lines have apparently been lost,—after 1312, 1417, 1696, 1719, 2094, 2293, 2695, 2840, 2960, 3057, 3134, 3365, 3395. Irregularities in rime are numerous, but in most cases easily emended.[4] The dialect is southeast Midland, with an intermixture of Northern forms.[5] The text has been edited by Wright (Percy Society for 1845, vol. XVI, pp. 1–118). For a collation of this edition with the manuscript, see Kölbing in *Englische Studien*, VI, p. 448 f. An analysis of the romance on the basis of this text appears in Clouston's *Book of Sindibād*, p. 327 f.

As.—MS. Asloan, in the possession of Lord Talbot de Malahide, Malahide Castle, Ireland,—denoted by *As*. For a general description of the manuscript (quoted from Chalmers),

---

[1] An edition of this manuscript by the lamented Dr. Robert Morris was announced by the E. E. T. S. many years ago; and an editor was advertised for for some time after Dr. Morris's death, but in the recent issues of the publications this advertisement no longer appears. It is the purpose of the present writer to prepare a critical edition of this text within the near future.

[2] For a general description of this manuscript, see the Cambridge *Catalogue*, I, p. 15 f.; Skeat, *Publications of E. E. T. S.*, vol. XXXVIII, p. XXIII f.; and Halliwell, *Manuscript Rarities of Cambridge*, p. 3.

[3] Morsbach, for some unknown reason, would place it earlier, "1300?"; see his *M. E. Grammatik*, p. 9.

[4] Lines 337–9 may be explained as a triplet, but it is better to suppose that a verse has been lost. A more probable example of the triplet in M. E. is found in *A*, 915–7.

[5] See Skeat, E. E. T. S., vol. XXXVIII, p. XXV, and Brandl, in *Paul's Grundriss*, II, 1, p. 635.

see Schipper's *Poems of Dunbar*, Vienna, 1891, Pt. 1, p. 5 f.[1] The text of the *Seven Sages* occupies ff. 167–209, and bears the title *The Buke of the sevyne Sagis*. According to Laing[2] the text is incomplete, extending to only about 2800 lines, and the twelfth and thirteenth stories are wanting entirely. It begins,

and ends,
> 'Ane Empriour in tymes bygane
> In Rome callit Dioclesiane—'
>
> 'Syne ȝeid till heuyn and sa do we
> Sayis all Amen for cherite.'

Its dialect is Scottish.[3] A complete transcript, made by D. Laing in 1826, exists in the University Library, Edinburgh. An edition, long ago promised by Varnhagen, is expected to appear shortly in the *Scottish Text Society Publications*.

2. *Interrelation of the Middle English Versions.*

With regard to the relationship of the Middle English versions there has been a variety of opinions, and, as in the case of the French versions, there has existed no little ignorance and error. The general tendency has been to consider any and all versions of the M. E. period independent translations from the French. This has been nowhere better demonstrated than in Petras's dissertation, where it has been boldly maintained that at least four of the M. E. versions (*A, C, F, D*) are unrelated save through a common foreign original. And while others have been more conservative than Petras, the prevailing opinion seems to have been that a majority at least of the M. E. group are independent of each other. It will be one of the results of this study, however, it is believed, to show that seven of the eight M. E. versions

---

[1] A further description, together with an extract containing the story *avis*, has recently appeared in *Englische Studien* (xxv, p. 321 f.), through the kindness of Prof. Varnhagen.

[2] *The Seven Sages in Scottish Metre* (Rolland), Edinburgh, 1837, p. xii.

[3] Chalmers says of it: "Evidently written by a Scotish versifier in the reign of James IV, as a number of Scotish terms occur, which would not have been introduced by a Scotish transcriber of an English work."

are ultimately related through a common M. E. parent version (x), and it is held not improbable that the eighth (As) is also thus related to x.

All the M. E. versions, however, do not represent the same line of tradition. One of the texts, D, as later shown, is a development from x, independent of the rest of the M. E. group, and Varnhagen holds that As was made directly from the Old French. The remaining versions fall together into one connected group, all related through a common original (y), which goes back to x, but which was not identical with it. This group will be designated as Y.

The close relationship of the texts which constitute this group Y is confirmed by evidence from all sides, but it can be no more effectively illustrated than by a comparative table of lines. For this purpose a line-for-line comparison of the section which the five most important texts of this group (A, Ar, E, B, C) have in common has been made, the comparison being restricted to identical lines and similar rimes, with the following results :[1]

(1) $A = 1816$ ll.

	Total ll.	Ident. ll.	Sim. rimes.
Ar	1916	234	722
E	1843	125	636
B	1934	154	537
C	2067	26	—[2]

(2) $Ar = 1916$ ll.

	Total ll.	Ident. ll.	Sim. rimes.
A	1816	234	722
E	1843	169	746
B	1931	137	646
C	2067	19	413

(3) $E = 1843$ ll.

	Total ll.	Ident. ll.	Sim. rimes.
A	1816	125	636
Ar	1916	169	746
B	1931	83	558
C	2067	11	352

(4) $B = 1931$ ll.

	Total ll.	Ident. ll.	Sim. rimes.
A	1816	154	537
Ar	1916	137	646
E	1843	83	558
C	2067	13	281

(5) $C = 2067$ ll.

	Total ll.	Ident. ll.	Sim. rimes.
A	1816	26	—[2]
Ar	1916	19	413
E	1843	11	352
B	1931	13	281

[1] An illustration of the method by which these figures have been arrived at may be found in the appendix to this study. F, owing to special features which are discussed below, is excluded from this comparison.

[2] Petras, p. 11, finds A and C, the entire texts being compared, to have 1096 similar rimes.

But this comparison, while valuable as far as it goes, serves only to show a connection between the texts compared; it does not suffice to show the nature of this connection. Accordingly, in addition to this, a comparison of motive or incident—as a safer basis for classification—has been made for the entire Middle English group; and it is by means of this, in the main, that our results as to the interrelation of the M. E. versions have been reached. The limits of this publication, however, preclude the submitting this except in part, so that only the tabulation for the story *vidua* (*Matron of Ephesus*) appears here.

(1) A certain knight had a wife. (*A, Ar, B, D* state that he was a *sheriff*.)	*A*	*Ar*	*E*	*B*	*C*	*F*	*D*	*A** 80, "un vicomte en Loherainne."
(2) They loved each other exceedingly. (*Ar* only relates that he loved her. In *F*, he will not permit her to go half a mile from him, "neither to church nor to cheping.")	*A*	(*Ar*)	*E*	*B*	*C*	*F*		*A**
(3) A new sharp knife is given them.	*A*	*Ar*	*E*	*B*	*C*			*A**
(4) While playing with this, he cuts her { in the thumb. in the womb. (*C*, in the finger; *F*, in the hand; *D* is silent as to part. *F* adds that the wife was paring a pear.)	*A*	*Ar*	*E*	*B*				*A**, "el pouce."
(5) For dole he dies on the morrow. (*F* adds that he asks for a priest before he dies.)	*A*	*Ar*	*E*		*C*		*D*	*A**
(6) This was great folly.	*A*	*Ar*	*E*	*B*				*A**

(7) He was richly buried on the morrow. (*B* does not specify that it was on the morrow. *E, B, C* state that this occurs after a mass. *D* adds that the place of burial was outside the city, since there were objections to his being buried within the city.)	*A*	*Ar*	*E*	(*B*)	*C*		(*D*)	*A**
(8) The wife refuses to leave the grave.	*A*	*Ar*	*E*	*B*	*C*	*F*	*D*	*A**
(9) Her friends try to comfort her.	*A*	*Ar*	*E*	*B*	*C*		*D*	*A**, "ses lignages."
(10) They suggest that she is young, and may marry again, and beget children.	*A*	*Ar*		*B*	*C*			(*A**)."jueneet bele." (No mention of marrying in *A**, but see *K* and the D'Ancona text.)
(11) She rejects their suggestions, assuring them that she will die on his grave. They are sorry.	*A*	*Ar*		*B*	*C*			*A** 81.
(12) They make for her a "logge" on the grave.	*A*	*Ar*	*E*	*B*	*C*			*A**, "une loge."
(13) Also, a fire. (*D*, she makes the fire herself. An addition of *D* is that she sends for her clothes.)	*A*	*Ar*	*E*		*C*		(*D*)	*A**
(14) Her friends leave her; she moans.	*A*	*Ar*	*E*	*B*	*C*		*D*	*A**
(15) On the same day three thieves have been taken. (*E*, on a day before; *B*, silent; *F*, one thief.)	*A*	*Ar*	(*E*)	(*B*)	*C*	(*F*)	*D*	*A**, "à celui jour."
(16) They were knights who had wasted the country, and had been hanged as soon as captured.	*A*	*Ar*	*E*	*B*	*C*			*A**

(17) A certain knight was to guard the bodies for the first night. (*A* adds that he was to watch for three nights.)	*A*	*Ar*	*E*	*B*	*C*	*F*	*D*	*A*,"un chevalier—la première nuit."
(18) Becoming cold, he spies the fire in the "churchhaw," goes thither, and finds the lady.	*A*	*Ar*	*E*	*B*	*C*	*F*	*D*	*A*, "cimetière."
(19) He asks to be let in.	*A*	*Ar*	*E*	*B*		*F*		*A** 82.
(20) She refuses his request. In *A* she swears by St. (John,—in *Ar, E, B*, by "St. Austyn.")	*A*	*Ar*	*E*	*B*	*C*			*A**
(21) He assures her that he will do her no harm, and that he is a knight.	*A*	*Ar*	*E*	*B*	*C*			*A** (*K* 3768, "Je sui Gerart le fil Guion;" also *D** 37.)
(22) She lets him in; he warms by the fire. (In *D* there is no mention of the wife's refusing to permit the knight to enter.)	*A*	*Ar*	*E*	*B*	*C*	*F*	*D*	*A**
(23) He sees her making dole, and tells her she is foolish to do so,—that she may yet marry some knight. She replies that he was so kind that she may not love any other. (*D* adds that she begins to love him when she finds him to be a knight; and that he lies with her.)	*A*	*Ar*	*E*	*B*	*C*			*A**
(24) By and by he thinks of his charge.	*A*	*Ar*	*E*	*B*	*C*			(*A**)
(25) And fearing guile, he rides fast to the gallows, only to find one of the bodies stolen. (*A, Ar, E, B*, he rides on a foal.)	*A*	*Ar*	*E*	*B*	*C*	*F*	*D*	*A** 83.

(26) He fears he will lose his advancement if unable to recover the body.	A	Ar	E	B	C		D	A*
(27) Bethinks himself that "wimmen couþe red."	A	Ar	E	B	C			A* (the order of 26-7 reversed in the French.)
(28) So going to the widow, he asks counsel of her.	A	Ar	E	B	C	F	D	A* (cf. K, 3817).
(29) She agrees to help him if he will marry her. (B, E, she proposes only that he be her "leman,"— he suggests matrimony. In C, she asks if he has a wife.)	A	Ar	E	B	C	F		A*
(30) This being agreed to, she advises that they dig up the body of her husband, which is done.	A	Ar	E	B	C	F	D	A*
(31) But the knight objects to hanging up the body.	A	Ar	E		C	F		A*
(32) The lady puts a rope round the neck of the corpse. (E, the knight does it.)	A	Ar	(E)	B	C	F		A*
(33) She draws the body up, and hangs it fast.	A	Ar			C	F		A*
(34) The knight is aghast at this.	A	Ar	E	B				
(35) The knight recalls that the thief had a wound in his head, and fears that the "guile may be perceived" unless the husband have a similar one; this the wife advises him to make with his sword.	A	Ar	E	B	C	F	D	A* 84, "une plaie en la teste."
(36) He declines to do it.	A	Ar	E	(B)	(C)		D	
(37) She asks for his sword, proposing to do it herself.	A	Ar	E	B	C	F		A*

(38) She smites with all her strength "amid the brayn." (In *D*, she wounds him with a knife.)	*A*	*Ar*	*E*	*B*	(*C*)	*F*	*D*	*A**
(39) The knight now knows her to be false.	*A*	*Ar*	*E*	*B*	*C*			
(40) He remembers that the thief's fore-teeth had been broken out. (*D*, *F*, in agreement with *A**, *K*, have *two* teeth; but see *D** 39, *toutes les dens*.)	*A*	*Ar*	*E*	*B*	*C*	(*F*)	(*D*)	*A**
(41) She proposes that he disfigure her husband in like manner, but he refuses.	*A*	*Ar*			*C*		*D*	(*A**)
(42) She does it herself with a stone. (In *A*, *Ar*, *E*, *B*, *F*, she knocks out *all* his teeth; in *D*, only *two*. *F* inserts here another disfiguration—the loss of two fingers. In *D*, the body is not hung up till after the mutilation.)	*A*	*Ar*	*E*	*B*	*C*	*F*	*D*	*A**
(43) The wife states that she has now won his love, which he denies, adding that he would marry her for no treasure, lest she serve him as she has served her lord.	*A*	*Ar*	*E*	*B*	*C*	*F*		(*A**)
(44) The sage wishes Diocletian such fortune if he do not respite the prince.	*A*	*Ar*	*E*	*B*	*C*	*F*	*D*	*A** 85.
(45) He asks that judgment be suspended till the morrow, when the prince will speak for himself.	*A*	*Ar*	(*E*)	*B*	*C*			*A**
(46) The emperor agrees to this, and the crowds disperse.	*A*	*Ar*		*B*	*C*		*D*	*A**

(47) The emperor goes to his bower; the empress "lours" on him. (*A*, *Ar* add that his "sergeants make solace" with him.)	*A*	*Ar*	*E*	*B*	*C*	*F*	*D*	*A**
(48) The emperor is brought abed *with riche baudekines.*	*A*	*Ar*						
(49) The empress is silent till the morrow.	*A*	*Ar*	*E*	*B*	*C*		*D*	
(50) When she asks if he has heard the "geste," etc., why men made a *feast of fools.*[1] (*Ar*, "How Rome was in great dread." *D* likewise makes no mention of the feast of fools.)	*A*	(*Ar*)	*E*	*B*	*C*		(*D*)	*A**, *K* 2347, "feste aus fox."

A.—*A* is naturally the most valuable of all Middle English versions, since it is found in the oldest manuscript which has come down to us, and doubtless in many respects best preserves the original. In view of its age one would at least hope to find in it either the parent English text or the closest representative of it, but a close collation with the remaining manuscripts shows that it is neither the one nor the other. It is not even a link in any one of the chains of development. This is established by the fact that *A* often abridges where all the other texts of *Y* are true to the French.[2]

There are, however, some features in which *A* appears to reflect the original more faithfully than any other member of its group. Thus, we find in *A* 666, "Deu vous doint bonjour" = *L* 15, "Diex vos doint bon jor," where none approximate *A* save *B* 652, "And sayde, deux vous garde bonjour;" or, in *A* 743, "The levedi stod *in pount tournis*"=

---

[1] For the origin of this feature, see Paris, *Romania*, IV, 128.

[2] This phenomenon does not seem to be confined to our text, but appears also in other poems of the Auchinleck MS., as has been already observed by Kölbing; cf. his *Arthour and Merlin*, IV, p. CLIII, and his *Bevis of Hamtoun*, E. E. T. S., Ex. Ser., LXV, p. XLI.

L 17, "sur le pont torneiz," where C reads "on a vice," and E, B, "in the castle on high." And there are sundry details of the original which A reproduces in common with only one other text; but these are easily explained by the circumstance of A's closer proximity in time to the parent text, in consequence of which it has suffered less from the ravages of time, or at the hand of the modernizer, than have some of the later texts.

The abridgments of the original which characterize A fall chiefly in the conclusions of certain stories. In fact it is a noticeable feature—due probably to the desire to avoid repetition—that it is almost entirely in the 'epilogaciouns' (as some of the H-texts name them) that A has made any serious alterations, while there is a very marked agreement, and only occasional freedom, exhibited in the body of its stories.

This tendency to abridge is manifest throughout the A-text. It is most violent, however, in the stories *aper, gaza, Virgilius*, and *avis*. Chief among the passages in other versions which find nothing corresponding in A, are the following: (1) *aper*, Ar, 1-20 = E 949-968 = B 933-948 = C 1041-1058 = L, p. 25; (2) *Virgilius*, Ar 1280-1288 = E 2204-2212 = B 2244-2252 = C 2370-2376 = L, p. 55; (3) *avis, Ar* 1433-1446 = E 2367-2372 = B 2401-2414 = L, p. 59.

There is, in addition to these, in the conclusion of *gaza*, a fourth passage which A abridges radically, and which, since it is a comparatively close paraphrase of the Old French, may be cited here as giving a graphic illustration of this peculiarity of A, and, at the same time, as showing once for all its unoriginality, and its subordinate importance in settling the question of the interrelation of the English versions. This passage is, in Ar, ll. 456-479; the corresponding lines are, in E 1401-1426, B 1393-1420, and C 1472-1490. Citation is made from Ar as best representing the lost text Y.

Ar 456 'Loude þei gonne on hym to crye,
　　And saide, lentylyon kyþe þy mastry,
　　Helpe þy disciple at þis nede.
　　þe master a-lyȝt þo of his stede,

L 34. 'Chascun li escria:
Ha! mestre, or pansez de vostre deciple.'
... 'et descent de son cheval.'

460 And grete þe Emperour on his kne. Unneþe wold he hym see. þe Emperour saide, þou fals man, Be hym þat al men-kynde wan, þou art fekell and fatour, 465 Losenger and eke traytour. A, why syr leue lord? So nas I neuer, saue þy word. Syr, þy gentyll wyue late us her, And with goddes helpe we schull us skor. 470 I ȝow toke my soñ to loke And for to tech hym on boke, And þou first bygan to tech, By-nome his tong and his spech, And tauȝt hym sith with mor stryf, 475 Ffor to nyme forth my wyf. ȝe schull wite þeir-of nouȝt; Bot when he is to deþe brouȝt, I schull dampne þe and þy feren 479 To drawe and honge by þe swyren.'	'... et s'en vient devant l'empereeur, si le salue: ... Li empereres respont au salu qui li a dit: Ja dex ne vos beneie.' 'Avoi! fet messires Lantules, pourcoi dites vos ce? ' Ge le vos dirai, fait li empereres, je vos avoie baillie mon fil à aprendre et à endoctriner, et la premiere doctrine que li avez faite, si est que vos li avez la parole tolue; l'autre qui veult prendre ma fame à force. Mes ja Dex ne vos en doint joir; et bien sachiez que tantost comme il sera morz, vos morroiz apres, et seroiz destruit ensement.'

As against this *A* has only the following lines (1387–92):

'And th' emperour wel sone he fond:
He gret him faire, ich understood. (= *Ar* 460)
Th' emperour saide, so God me spede, (= *Ar* 462)
Traitour, the schal be quit thi mede!
For mi sones mislerning,
Ye schulle habbe evil ending!'

Other less important omissions occur in the conclusions to *aper* and *puteus*: *aper*—the people invoke the master to help his disciple (*L* 25, *C* 1064, *E*, *B*); *puteus*—the empress threatens, on learning of the respite of the prince, to leave on the morrow. *Ar* 624–5, "And saide scho wold away at morowe. Nai dame, he saide, ȝef God it wyll...." = *L* 38, "je m'en irai le matin. Non ferois, dame .... se dieux plest." The same incident is omitted in the *A*-text of *avis*; cf. *L* 59, *Ar* 1440–1.

In the body of the stories, as already observed, this tendency is not nearly so marked. There is in fact no significant feature of the stories of the original which has been preserved in any other English version that does not appear also in A. The nearest approaches to such are the following, both from the story *Roma*: (1) An old wise man ($= A*$ 86, "un home viel et ancien. . . .") makes the proposition that the city be put in charge of seven sages, a bit of detail which is omitted by no other English version; (2) after these sages have kept the city for a month, the food supply is exhausted; cf. Ar, E, B, C, F, and $A*$ 86, "vitaille failli à ceuls." In addition to these there are certain other minor details in which one or more of the related English versions preserve the French more closely. For example, in *medicus* (A 1149), Ypocras pierces the ton in *1000* places, as against Ar (208), E, B, F, which agree with L 28, -c- *broches*. Likewise in *Virgilius*, A (1977-8) translates the O. F. "arc de coivre et une sajete, bien entesse" (L 50) as "arblast .... and quarel taisand," while the remaining members of group Y render more literally *bow* and *arrow;* in *sapientes*, C, Ar, E, B have the masters ask Merlin his name, in agreement with L 60, "et li demandèrent commant il avoit à non," where A abridges; to which add that A makes no mention of the divine service at the burial of the husband in *vidua*, where E, B, C, fall in with $A*$ 80, and that in the same story, A (2618) has the knight come to the gallows to watch *three* nights, while Ar, E, B, C fall together in their adherence to the French—$A*$ 81, "la première nuit," and we have the sum of A's noteworthy variations within the body of its stories.

Additions in A are even less numerous. An occasional extra couplet (so far as the evidence of the remaining English versions goes) now and then crops out, as *e. g.*, 645-8, and we also find here and there additional details, such as (1) in *Virgilius*, where the poor, in addition to warming themselves at the magician's wonderful fire, are represented as also preparing their food by it (A 1973); and as (2) in *sapientes*, Herod is described as the richest man in Christendom (A 2340),—neither of which appears in any other text, whether English or Romance. But such additions are very few in number, and, in any case, too insignificant to play a prominent part in solving the problem in hand. They are, nevertheless, confirmatory of the evidence already adduced, with which they unite in demonstrating conclusively the unoriginality of A.

We have, then, in A a secondary development from the lost y. It cannot have been based on any manuscript of which any other text of Y is a close transcript, since it preserves the original in some places more faithfully than any other M. E. text. On the other hand, it cannot have been the source of any of the known M. E. manuscripts, since all these preserve features of the French which A omits.

Ar.—Nearest to A stands the fragmentary text from MS. Arundel 140. This version, while most important as representing in all probability the lost y more closely than any other known text, has been singularly neglected by former investigators. Petras makes no mention of it, whence we draw the inference that he was unacquainted with it. And apparently the only notice which has been accorded it, beyond Varnhagen's several references to it,[1] is that of Ward in his *Catalogue of Romances* (II, p. 224 f.). From a comparison of the introductory lines of *Ar* with the corresponding passages in A, E, C, Ward observed that its affinities seemed closest with E; and this indeed holds for the conclusions of several of the stories (Ward deals with a conclusion; cf. our parallelling of lines for *medicus*, in Appendix), where A has been seen to be often free, and where Ar, in consequence, frequently agrees more closely with any other text than with A. It does not hold, however, as regards the stories themselves, where E yields the first place to A.

Except in these conclusions, Ar agrees with A very closely. Their intimate relation is evident at once from our line-for-line statistics on p. 44. Of the 1916 lines of the Ar-section ($= A$ 1816), 234 are identical with lines in A, and there are

---

[1] First referred to in his *Eine Ital. Prosaversion d. Sieben Weisen*, p. XI, and later in his review of Petras, *Eng. Stud.*, X, p. 279.

722 similar rimes. Next comes *E* (1843 ll.) with 169 identical lines and 746 similar rimes,—a slightly larger percentage of rimes than for *A*, and an apparent discrepancy, which is, however, easily reconciled by the fact of *A*'s characteristic curtailments; *B* (1931 ll.) has 137 lines identical with *Ar* and 646 like rimes, and *C*, which comes last, has only 19 lines identical and 413 similar rimes.

But the closer relationship of *Ar* to *A* develops conclusively only from a comparison of details. Here, while a careful collation of *Ar* with all other members of *Y* reveals no noteworthy bit of detail in common with any other single text when contrasted with *A*, there are several interesting and significant agreements of *Ar* with *A* against the rest of *Y*. Among these are the following: (1) *A* 1462, " Ich wille bicome wod and wilde," which is identical with *Ar* 552; in *E* 1498, the empress (who is speaking here) seeks to slay herself (cf. *L* 36, " seroie-je morte "). (2) *A* 1580, " And he com als a leopard " = *Ar* 668, " Þane cam he rynnyng as a lyvarde." (3) *A* 1588, " Bihote hem pans an handfolle " = *Ar* 676, " Behote heme pens a pours full." (4) *A* 2396, "Al to loude thou spak thi latin " = *Ar* 1518, " To loude þou spake þy latyn." (5) *A* 2744, " Withe riche baudekines i-spredde " = *Ar* 1868, " With rich cloþes all byspred." None of these verses have anything corresponding in any other English text. Doubtless some of them are only accidental, but such cannot be the case with all. Their evidence is well supported by such further agreements as in *senescalcus*, where *A* and *Ar* unite in retaining the *twenty marks* of the original, other M. E. texts varying, or as in *vidua* where these two agree in that the wife is cut in the *womb*, while *E*, *B* preserve the French—in the *thumb* (*A** 80, *el pouce*), *C* states that the wounded part is a *finger*, *E* the *hand*, and *D* is indefinite. Of these agreements there can be only one explanation, namely in the assumption of a connection between the two texts. What the nature of this relation is, however, can be best determined after a collection of corresponding data for the other manuscripts.

In comparing the remaining texts with *Ar*, one is at once struck with the remarkable agreement of *B*, *E* with *A*, *Ar*. These four versions have a number of features in common which do not survive in *C*, *F*, or *D*. Thus (1) in *gaza*, the son stabs himself in the *thigh* (= *L* 33, *en la cuisse*), where *C*, *F* are free, the one reading *cheke*, the other *honde*. (2) In *senescalcus*, the king falls sick "by God's vengeance" (not in *L*; also omitted by *C*, *D*,—*F* omitting the entire story). (3) Again in the same story, the king offers *twenty marks* or *pounds* for a lady to lie with (= *L* 40, *xx mars*), where *C* reads *ten pounds*, and *D* simply "gold and silver." And this is still more apparent in a line-for-line collation, as is sufficiently demonstrated in the Appendix.

At the same time, also, one cannot but remark certain occasional agreements of *Ar* with *E*, *B* in opposition to *A*. For instance, (1) the king in *senescalcus*, with the former, has great delight in women, where *A* on the contrary, in agreement with the O. F., as also with *C*, *D*, describes him as disdaining women above all things (*L* 39, "Il desdaingnoit fame seur toutes riens"). And (2) in *sapientes*, the sages in *Ar*, *E*, *B* ask respite for *seven* days, where *A*, *C* give *fourteen* days, *F* 12, *L* 4–8, and *K* 15. Likewise (3) the servants of the king in *sapientes* dig under his bed "four feet or five" in *Ar*, *E*, *B*, while *A* makes no mention of the distance, but says ten or twelve men dig; so *L* 62, *xx homes*. To which is to be added (4) the agreement of *Ar*, *E*, *B* in having the husband in *vidua* (*Ar* 1756) swear by *St. Austyne;*—by *St. Johain* in *A* (2630). Nevertheless, these are not of such a nature as to contradict the classification of *Ar* with *A*, but merely indicate that in such cases, *Ar* best preserving the original, independence has been asserted by the poet of *A*.

But in view of these and of *A*'s frequent abridgments, we cannot look for the basis of *Ar* in *A*, nor—as it is hardly necessary to add, after the citation of textual agreements with

A—in *E* or *B*,—and still less, for even more obvious reasons, in *C* or *F.* The marked agreement of *Ar* with *A*, however, begets the assumption of a development of the former, parallel with the latter, from a common source *r*, through which they both go back to *y.*

Certain agreements of *Ar* with *E* against all other versions including *A* (treated more at length under *E*) are not altogether easy to reconcile, but owing to *Ar*'s nearness to other texts—*A* in particular—as against *E*, it is impossible to consider *Ar* as derived from it; we are led rather to the converse assumption, of a partial connection, or contamination, of *E* with *Ar*, or, in more likelihood, with the latter's immediate source *r.*

That *Ar* so far as it goes, best preserves the lost M. E. original is borne out on all sides: (1) by its close agreement with the texts *A* and *E*, which otherwise best reproduce this source; (2) by the fact that *F* in the last four stories (in which we should expect a close adherence to its original) is closer to it than to any other text; and (3) that while *A*, especially, and *E*, *B*, in a less degree, often add or omit lines, *Ar* almost never adds, and in only rare cases abridges.[1]

However, that no manuscript which has survived was based on *Ar* follows from its occasional freedom, as *e. g.*, (1) its rimes to 171-2, 227-8, 463-4, etc., which are parallelled by no other text, and (2) in *Roma* the names of *Julius* and *July*, —where all other texts better preserve the *Genus* (Janus) and *January* of the French.

E.—With the exception of *Ar*, the Egerton MS. would be of most value in preparing a normalized text, since it next best preserves the original, and especially since it is complete.

The value of *E* is considerably impaired, however, by the fact that its author—or more probably its scribe—has made an unusual number of textual abridgments,—as a rule for

---

[1] The only addition in the first 1900 ll. is 1871-2:

'When day bygane to sprynge,
And þe foules mery to synge.'

single couplets only, yet in a few cases for a half-dozen or more lines. Some of these are the following: (1) after 996 = *A* 991-2, (2) 1024 = *A* 1019-20, (3) 1216 = *A* 1211-2, (4) 1400 = *A* 1385-6, (5) 1500 = *A* 1465-6, (6) 1530 = *A* 1500-1, (7) 1558 = *A* 1529-30, (8) 1578 = *A* 1549-50, (9) 1646 = *A* 1615-6, (10) 1652 = *A* 1623-4, (11) 1662 = *A* 1633-4, (12) 1784 = *A* 1749-50, etc., and, most radical of all, (13) after 2472 = *A* 2424 f., where ten lines have been lost.[1] In consequence of this, *E* is somewhat shorter than either of the other complete texts, *B* and *C*. For the 2564 lines of the Arundel fragment, it has only 2365; and this number in reality should be reduced 18 lines, since the couplets with which *E* heads nine of its stories, and which have been included in this numbering, did not belong to the original, it is safe to assume, and should not, for purposes of comparison, be regarded as part of the text.

But beyond these slight abridgments, the author of *E* has, in the handling of his original, exhibited almost no independence. One looks in vain for such abridgments as characterize *A*, as also for significant additions such as are found in *F* and *C*. Excepting such occasional freedom as the assigning to the incident in *Roma* the date of the first of January, and the changing of the *barber* in *tentamina* into a *borowe*—a scribal error, doubtless—we shall find scarcely one other feature exclusively peculiar to *E*, until we have reached almost the end of the poem, when the poet for once appears to assert his independence, and we have in consequence the very interesting addition that—

'―― whenne that his fadyr dede was,
He lete make a nobylle plas,

[1] The additions are less numerous. Among those which are parallelled by no more than one other text, or are peculiar to *E*, are (1) 986-7 (after *A* 974), (2) 1015-6 (a. *A* 1012), (3) 1245-6 (a. *A* 1238), (4) 1621-2 = *A* 1591-2, (5) 1693-6 (a. *A* 1664), (6) 1761-2 (a. *A* 1726), (7) 1809-10 (a. *A* 1780), (8) 2097-2103 (a. *A* 2068), (9) 2291-4 (a. *A* 2246), and (10) 2349-51 (a. *A* 2298).

> And a fayre abbeye he lete begynne,
> And vii. schore monkys brought thereyn,
> And euyr more to rede and synge
> For hys fadyr with-owte lesynge.' (8561-6)

All other important variations in E are repeated in some one or more of the related M. E. versions. The agreement here is closest with B and Ar. Its near relation to the latter has already been shown, and it has been pointed out that there are features in which the two are alone; and there are also cases in which the two are alone in textual abridgments: *e. g.* Ar 227-8 $= E$ 1171-2. It has also been seen under Ar, that B in several instances falls in with E, Ar, as against A, C, F.

It remains to point out some of the motives common to E, B versus the remaining texts of Y. The most important of these are the following: (1) *arbor*—lords and ladies begin to weep when they see the prince led forth to be hanged; (2) *arbor*—Bancyllas assures the emperor that the prince will recover his speech; (3) *sapientes*—both omit the detail of A, Ar, C that Merlin declines the offer of money made by the man whose dream he has interpreted; (4) *vidua*—the wife is cut in the *thumb*, where other texts have variously *womb*, *finger*, and *hand*; as also (5) *vidua*—the knight's disregarding the widow's suggestion that he knock out her husband's teeth; (6) *Roma*—the sage who makes the proposition for saving Rome is called *Junyus* (A, C, F, *Gemes*; Ar, *Julius*; D, *Gynever*). In several of these, to wit 3, 4, 5, it will be observed, E, B are truest to the French.

Such evidence as this precludes the thought of a basis of E in Ar, but in view of the agreements between the two already noted, and, especially, of the fact that there is a greater number of Ar-lines than of B-lines identical with E's (cf. p. 44), it does not seem improbable—though I am unable to prove it—that the author of E has known and been partly influenced by Ar.

On the other hand there is abundant evidence of an all but immediate connection between B and E: (1) in the agreements in details just cited, and (2) in the textual omissions and additions which the two have exclusively in common. Thus, of the thirteen E-omissions collected above, six (1, 7, 9, 10, 11, 12) are also in B; and of the ten additions cited in the foot-note (p. 58), three (1, 8, 9) are common to B,—or a total of 9 out of 23—a remarkable showing when it is borne in mind that in ten of these cases E is alone, agreeing in only one case (abridgments—9) with any other text than B.

Despite these, however, E cannot have been based on B, since it preserves in agreement with other texts—notably Ar—features of the original which B omits.

In the next section it will be shown, also, that B was not based on E, and it will be further demonstrated that the two are related through a common source.

B.—The Balliol text, like E, is complete and of late composition. The analogy between the two does not stop here, however; there are many things which bind them together, not only when looked at externally, but also from an interior point of view. One of the most striking phenomena which they have in common, and which one cannot but remark in comparing them with Ar and the remaining Y-texts, is the tendency to reverse the order of words, or to substitute synonymous or analogous expressions,—in consequence of which the identity of the line and often the rime is destroyed. This is equally as prominent in B as in E, if not more so. In B especially, the change of epithet often flows, one feels, from a desire to modernize, rather than from a conscious effort, as might be supposed, to conceal the source.

In some other respects, however, B and E are very unlike. For instance, while it is characteristic of E to drop out one or more couplets for every column, B is exceptionally free from such slight curtailments, while its additional couplets are comparatively numerous.[1] Moreover, while E is at first

---

[1] In the first 1000 lines of the part selected for a line-for-line comparison (= B 933–1951), B has 16 couplets which do not appear in any other manuscript, and which were accordingly, in large part in all probability, its own additions. E, on the contrary, has only 4, or one-fourth as many (1015–6, 1245–6 and 1693–6).

close to the original—more so by far in the first thousand
lines than anywhere else—and becomes more and more free, *B*
exhibits just the reverse tendency, and we find it in the last
third of the poem textually almost as close to the original
as is *E*.

As regards incident, *B* is usually more free than any
one of the texts so far treated. Its chief variations—in the
nature of additions largely—are the following: (1) *aper*—
the herd fills both *arms* and *sleeves* (later *laps*) with the haws;
A, E, laps = *L* 23, *girons*; *C, D, hood*. (2) *medicus*—the illegitimate
father of the sick prince, called in the remaining
members of *Y* either the *earl* or the *king of Naverne* (= *L* 27,
li quens de Namur) is not named. (3) *puteus*—besides the
feature peculiar to *Y*, viz. that the burgess would only marry
some one from a distance, *B* adds that he also would marry
no poor woman,—with the additional information that he
already had had two wives. The feature of *A, E, Ar*, that
he made a covenant with the bride's father, does not appear in
B. (4) *senescalcus*—while in the remaining texts the steward
is banished, in *B* he is put to death—and *by pouring molten
silver and lead down his throat*. This incident, which constitutes
the most violent freedom of *B*, is apparently borrowed
from *Virgilius*, where Crassus dies a similar death. The
punishment in either case is fitted to the crime. (5) *tentamina*—the
wife wishes to love the *parish priest*, where *A, Ar,
E, F, C* have simply *priest* = *L, provoire* (but see *D** 27,
Messire Guillaume le chappelain de la parroise). (6) *sapientes*—
they meet with the old man after *two days;* other texts not
definite as to time. (7) *Roma*—the town is put in charge of
two wise men; in other texts it is *seven*. (8) *inclusa*—the
knight has travelled only *one* month before he comes into
the land of his lady; according to other M. E. versions it is
three months (*K, D*, A** 89, *trois semaines;* but cf. Varnhagen's
Ital. Prosaversion, p. 36, *tre mesi*. (9) *inclusa*—the
wife's ring had been given her as a New Year's gift,—an
invention of *B*.

But while B has thus many features peculiar to itself, it possesses very few exclusively peculiar to itself and any one other text,—a circumstance which renders the problem of its relations somewhat difficult of solution. We may resort, however, to the verse-omissions or additions, and it is significant here that the evidence from motive-comparison (submitted already under E) which pointed to a relation with E, receives very strong confirmation. In almost every instance in which B agrees in an addition or omission with only one other text, this text is E. Thus, in the first thousand lines of the constant element in $Y (= B$ 934 f.), there is a total of ten such variations, of which nine are in agreement with E—the tenth being with C, an agreement which can only be explained as a coincidence or, at least, as signifying nothing. The agreements with E, however, cannot well be accidental. They offer strong confutation of the evidence of the line-collation (p. 44), which seems to indicate a closer relationship with A or Ar.

That B was not based on either of the latter—A, Ar—follows from the fact that it preserves certain features of the original (cf. 3, 4, 5 of motive-agreements of E, B, p. 59) which they have either lost or altered.

And that both B and E go back to y independently of each other is rendered improbable in the highest degree by their agreements in omissions and additions. We are forced then to the assumption of the existence at some time of a manuscript—denoted by s—which served as the common source of B and E.

F.—There is no one of the M. E. texts of the *Seven Sages* which has been more imperfectly reported than that contained in the Cambridge University MS. Ff, II, 38. Wright as early as 1845 was acquainted with this version, and printed in the introduction (p. LXX) to his edition of D the opening lines, but vouchsafed no further description of the text than that it presented many different readings from A and was much mutilated. And Petras, on the basis of this description, and with the aid of about 190 lines of the text, has inclined to the view that *F* is nearer to *C* than to any other M. E. version.[1] Neither Wright nor Petras, however, has made reference to the description of Halliwell in his *Thornton Romances* (Camden Society Publications, xxx, p. XLII f.), and both were evidently ignorant of it.

The description of Halliwell is the most reliable which has up to this time appeared; yet in one or two instances it, too, is inaccurate. For example, the thirteenth story of *F* has been overlooked entirely; again it implies that there is only one new story introduced into this version,—the one which he prints on p. XLIII f. In reality there is a second story in *F* which is peculiar to it,—the ninth story, to which Halliwell gives the name *The Squyer and his Borowe*. This tale is complete and runs as follows:

'Hyt was a squyer of thys contre,
1115 And full welbelouyd was he.
Yn dedys of armys and yn justyng [145 b.]
He bare hym beste yn hys begynnyng.
So hyt befelle he had a systur sone,
That for syluyr he had nome,
1120 He was put yn preson strong,
And schulde be dampned, *and* be hong.
The squyer faste thedur can gon,
And askyd them swythe anon
What þyng he had borne a-way;
1125 And they answeryd, *and* can say,
He had stolen syluyr grete plente;
Therfore hangyd schulde he bee.
The squyer hym profurd, permafay,
To be hys borowe tyll a certen day,
1130 For to amende that he mysdede,
Anon they toke hym yn that stede,
And bounde hym faste fote *and* honde
And caste hym yn-to preson stronge.
They let hys cosyn go a-way
1135 To quyte hym be a certen day.
Grete pathes then used he,
And men he slewe grete plente.
Moche he stale *and* bare a-way,
And stroyed the contre nyght *and* day.

[1] See his dissertation, p. 31. Cf. also Varnhagen, in his review of Petras, *Englische Studien*, x, p. 281 f.

> 1140 Bot upon þe squyer þoght he nothyng
> That he yn preson lefte lyeng,
> So that tyme came as y yow say,
> But for the squyer came no paye.
> He was hanged on a galowe tree.
> 1145 For hym was dole and grete pyte,
> When the noble squyer was slon, [145 c.]
> For hym morned many oon.
> That odur robbyd and stale moche þyng,
> And sethyn was hangyd at hys endyng.
> 1150 Thus schall be-tyde of þe, syr Emperour,
> And of thy sone, so gret of honour.'

Otherwise Halliwell's description is characterized by the strictest accuracy, and leaves no room for the assumption, apparently made by Petras, of an identity in the order of stories between F and the remaining M. E. versions.

The correct order of stories in F is as follows: (1) *arbor*, (2) *puteus*, (3) *aper*, (4) *tentamina*, (5) *gaza* (end of), (6) *vidua*, (7) *Riotous Son* (beginning of), (8) *canis* (end of), (9) *Squyer and Borowe*, (10) *avis*, (11) *sapientes*, (12) *medicus*, (13) *Roma*, (14) *inclusa*, and (15) *vaticinium*. Eight stories then (1, 3, 5, 10, 11, 13, 14, 15) retain their usual order. The two new stories, 7 and 9, supplant *senescalcus* and *Virgilius*, taking their respective order. For the remaining five stories, 2 changes place with 8, 4 with 12, 6 with 2, 8 with 4, and 12 with 6. For this order there is no parallel either in other English or in foreign versions, and there can be little doubt that it was original with the F-redactor.

In content, also, F is very unique. In some cases the original story has been altered almost beyond recognition. This alteration consists largely in textual abridgments, but it is also very evident in the many new incidents that have been introduced.

The introduction, in contradistinction to the stories of the first part, is but slightly abridged. It exhibits several more or less interesting variations, but the only one of any significance is the assigning to the king's steward the distinction (accorded the king's retinue in the other texts) of making the petition which saves the prince's life the first day.

> 'Then come forthe the steward,
> And seyde, syr, thys was not forward,
> When that y holde the thy londe,
> When ii. kynges bade þe batell with wrong,
> And then þou swere be heuen kyng
> Thou schuldest neuer warne me myn askyng.
> Geue me thy sones lyfe to-day,
> Yentyll Emperour, y the pray,
> And let hym to-morowe be at þy wylle,
> Whethur þou wylt hym saue or spylle.
> I graunt the, seyde the Emperour,
> To geue hym lyfe be seynt sauyour.' (380–391)

Arbor is very much abridged, the story proper comprising only twenty lines. There is no mention of the burgess's going away from home, nor of the trimming away of the branches of the old tree.

Of *canis* only a short fragment is left, for which compare Halliwell, *Thornton Romances*, p. XLIV.

Aper has to do with a "swynherde" who has lost a "boor," and who

> '—— durste not go home to hys mete
> For drede hys maystyrs wolde hym bete,'

but climbs a tree, and is making a repast of acorns when the wild-boar of the forest comes up.

Medicus is one of the last four stories,—hence agrees faithfully with its original.

Only the conclusion of *gaza* has been preserved.

Puteus has undergone radical alteration: (1) The curfew of the original is omitted. Instead of it there is a law in Rome that whosoever shall be found away from home at night with any woman other than his wife shall be stoned to death on the morrow. (2) The lover here is a "squire of great renown." (3) The burgess uses a rope in trying to get his wife from the well. (4) He has already had two wives before his marriage with the one who figures here. This feature has been transplanted from the introduction to *tentamina*, where it properly belongs.

Senescalcus and *Virgilius* do not appear in *F*.

Tentamina is characterized by the addition of a fourth trial, the killing of the knight's hawk. Other features are (1) the assigning to the wife the office of the gardener in the first trial (she fells the tree, and sets "dokys *and* nettuls" in its stead), (2) the omission of mention of the church as the meeting-place of mother and daughter, and (3) the transference to *puteus* of the 'two-wives'-feature.

Avis, though textually free, contains no unusual details other than (1) that the lover is a priest, and (2) that the wife is killed by the enraged husband.

In *sapientes*, however, there are several striking variations: (1) The sages build a "horde-house" just above the city gate, which renders the emperor blind whenever he tries to pass it in going out of the city. (2) There is no mention of Merlin's first dream-interpretation, a feature in which *F* agrees with *D*,—an agreement, however, which can only be accidental since *F* contains the search for and meeting of the sages with Merlin, which we find no hint of in *D*.

Vidua has the following peculiar features: (1) The husband will never let his wife go a half-mile from him, "neither to church nor to cheping." (2) The wife is paring a *pear* when she cuts herself. (3) There is mention of only *one* thief, and he is not alluded to as a knight. (4) A "pyke and spade" are used in digging up the corpse. (5) In addition to the mutilations usually recorded, *F* adds a fourth,—the cutting off of *two fingers* which the knight claimed that the thief had lost.

The last three stories, *Roma*, *inclusa*, and *vaticinium*, offer essential agreement in detail with the other texts of *Y*.

The variations of *F* are thus seen to be very numerous. Yet, significant though many of them are, they tell only half the story. The whole truth is revealed only when it is considered that along with these, and partly consequent upon them, the length of the poem has been reduced by about one-third, or to little more than 2500 lines.

And what is most noteworthy about this abridgment is that it is not carried through the entire text, but extends only through the eleventh story. Up to the conclusion of this story the greatest freedom prevails, old incidents are rejected and new ones introduced at will, and, again resorting to figures for forcible illustration, the text is reduced from a normal 2500 lines to scarcely more than 1000.[1] In the remaining four stories, however, there is, as has been seen, close agreement with the remaining texts of Y.

How to account for this wholesale mutilation to which F has subjected its original is not an easy problem. One would think of a basis for the first part in oral accounts, but this is rendered extremely improbable by the fact that throughout this part there is frequent agreement of rimes, and not unusual identity of lines, with other M. E. versions. Or again, there is a possibility that F was made from some very fragmentary manuscript, but there is no substantial basis for this supposition, and the changed order of stories is distinctly against it. The most probable view, by far, seems to be that the poet had before him a complete manuscript, which, for some reason, possibly to conceal his source, he has for the first eleven stories arbitrarily altered; and that beginning with the twelfth story, having grown tired of his task, he has for the remaining stories reproduced his original with fidelity.

With the acceptance of this explanation, the problem of F's relationship is rendered comparatively simple; for, if the variations of the first part are attributable to the poet, this part is of little value for purposes of comparison, and we are accordingly restricted to the last part as the basis for any investigation.

For this part there is comparatively close textual agreement with E, B, C, Ar, and A (the last two unfortunately fragmentary here in part). No single important detail and a very

[1] For the corresponding part, E has 2593 lines, and B, 2658.

small percentage of the rimes have been changed, while lines identical with one or more of the other texts are numerous. The agreement is closest with Ar as a rule, with E next in order; thus, for the 845 lines (F 1440-2285) which the three texts have in common, only 53 lines of F are identical with lines in E, while the corresponding figure for Ar is 116. Again, for this section Ar has agreement with F in 26 couplets which do not appear in E (F 1476-7, 1490-1, 1694-5 [B, A], 1714-5, 1726-31, 1738-9, 1754-5, 1774-7, 1790-1, etc). But despite this affinity with Ar, F cannot have been based on it, for in one case (F 2280-1) Ar lacks a couplet which both E and F have preserved, and in other cases, it has made independent additions (cf. Ar 1896-7, 2374-7, 2384-5). This slight evidence is everywhere well supported: on the one hand we find B, though much farther removed than E or Ar, nearest F (cf. B 1095 = F 1578); again A will be found to be nearest (cf. A 997 = F 1464, A 1016 = F 1487, A 1048 = F 1518, A 1088-9 = F 1553-4); while in other instances several will agree as against Ar (cf. A 2762 = B 2848 = F 1679, and A 2751 = E 2762 = B 2833 = F 1662).

In the face of this otherwise contradictory evidence, it is impossible to find the source of F in any *one* known manuscript. At the same time there is nothing to indicate a partial basis on any two of them, since some exclusive agreements with each of the other closely related texts are found. On the contrary, the evidence from all sides combines to show that F goes back to y independently of any other known manuscript.

C.—Petras, although he showed a close agreement of C with A—52 lines identical and 1296 with similar rimes—classed it apart from A, and as only related with it through a common O. F. source.[1] His own figures, however, as Varnhagen has already pointed out, justify quite another conclusion; for it is inconceivable that two independent translations from a foreign source should have 52 out of about 2500 lines identical, or 1300 with like rimes. The rather are

---

[1] See his dissertation, p. 21.

we to conclude that *C* is ultimately based on the ultimate common original of *A, Ar, E, B, F,* and belongs with them to group *Y*.

Of all M. E. texts *C* is the fullest and, from a literary point of view, the most perfect. At the same time it is, with the exception of *F*, the freest of the texts which comprise *Y*. This freedom, however, does not consist in the changed order of stories nor the wholesale mutilation of text which characterize *F*; nor is it violent or spasmodic. It flows from an independence or individuality of a much higher type, which neither eliminates old motives nor introduces new ones of a startling nature, but which contents itself, on the one hand, with a slight variation of the episode (generally in the nature of additions), on the other, with the enlargement and embellishment of the often more or less lifeless language of its original,— in both cases with the purpose of heightening the poetic effect. So that, while we see in *A* the most important of the M. E. texts from an historical viewpoint, in *Ar* the most faithful representative of the lost *y*, we have in *C* preëminently the most perfect *poem*, holding, as it does, in language, style, and metre, the first place in the early English group.

As regards fidelity to the original, as already suggested, *C* does not occupy a very high rank. Its variations, however, consist rather in amplification than in invention, as is well illustrated by the fact that, while 600 additional lines have been interwoven into the text, there are only the following noteworthy variations of incident : (1) The step-mother in bringing about the prince's downfall seeks counsel and assistance from a witch (297). (2) In *arbor*, the tree with which the story deals is a *pineapple-tree; A, E, B, F* read *pynnote-tree,* and *D, apple-tree.* (3) The queen in *medicus* states that it has been *twelve* years since the Earl of Naverne had visited her (1167) ; other texts indefinite. (4) The patient in the same story is advised to " Ete beres fless *and* drink þe bro " (1184). *A, Ar, E, B,* " beef's flesh with the broth " (*E,* " with the blood "); *L* 27, *char de buef.* (5) There is mention of only *two* clerks in *gaza*, where the remaining English and the French texts have *seven*, five of whom are stationed away from the city (1319). (6) In the same story the father alone goes into the tower Cressent, while in the other texts both father and son go (1340). (7) In *tentamina*, the history of each of the two deceased wives is related separately; in other texts it is simply stated that the husband had survived two wives (1879). (8) In the same story, also, it will be noted that only the right arm of the wife is bled. (9) In *Virgilius*, the two brothers themselves fill the two "forcers"; elsewhere the King has them filled. Other variations here are the changed order of incident in burying the treasure, and the omission of the name of the Emperor (Crassus). (10) There is, in *avis*, no mention of a maid as assisting the faithless wife. (11) The lord of the castle in *inclusa* is playing chess when the knight rides up (3294). (12) The son in *vaticinium* learns of the whereabouts of his father through a vision (4135).

We may judge from this enumeration how faithfully C has reproduced the subject-matter of the original. It has altered very few details, and none radically, while no single significant feature, either from the body or from the end of its stories, has been omitted; at the same time, only an occasional bit of detail has been added,—a remarkable showing, indeed, when the large increase in the number of lines is considered.

But there is more specific evidence of C's fidelity to its original. There are certain details in which it appears to give a more faithful reflex of the Old French than any other M. E. text. Thus, in *aper*, the boar on reaching the tree finds "hawes ferly fone" (987); cf. L 23, "s'il se merveille mult durement de ce qu'il ne pot autretant trover des alies comme il soloit faire devant." According to other M. E. versions the boar finds no haws at all. Another illustration may be had from *inclusa*, where C (3264) preserves the *Hongrie* of the French (A* 89) as the land into which the knight finally comes in search of his lady; M. E. variants are *Pletys* in Ar, and *Poyle* in E, F, and D.

And there are also instances in which *C* is in agreement with only one other text in its preservation of the French: (1) With *A* in its rendering *blanche leuriere* (*K* 2604; *L* 45, only *leurière*) by *gray bitch*, where *Ar, E, B* render *greyhound, F* simply *hound*. (2) With *F* in giving, in *Roma*, the information as to the origin of the word *January* at the beginning of the Janus-episode; other M. E. versions, where they preserve this detail, depart from the O. F. order in placing it at the conclusion of the story.

It is to these facts in the main that we have to resort to determine *C*'s immediate relations; for the theory of a direct translation from the O. F. can no longer be defended in the face of the evidence from a comparison of rimes, etc. From this comparison it is evident that *C* is nearly related to the other versions of group *Y*. That it cannot have been based on any one of them, however, follows from its agreements (just cited) with the French where the remaining M. E. texts are free. And this also derives confirmation from the features which it has exclusively in common with only one M. E. version and the O. F., for neither of the two M. E. versions in point here (*A* and *F*) can possibly have been its original.

We have, accordingly, to assume for *C* an independent basis in the lost text *y*. Whether one or more manuscripts intervene between *C* and *y* cannot be determined so long as they are not forthcoming; in any case there seems nothing to support Varnhagen's proposition (*Eng. Stud.*, x, p. 280) of a " mündliche Ueberlieferungsstufe " between the two.

D.—Version *D*, as compared with the texts so far considered, is unique, and cannot be classed with them in group *Y*. Though it is written in the same metre as the remaining M. E. versions, and while it preserves, also, the *A*-order of stories, it differs from each and every text of *Y* much more radically than any one of these differs from any other. And so great has this difference seemed that scholars have been unanimous in assuming for *D* an immediate basis in the Old French. The thought of a near kinship with any other M. E.

version appears never to have been entertained. Wright's testimony is to the effect that "The two English metrical versions (by which he meant A and D) are altogether different compositions; but . . . . were evidently translated from the same original. . . ."[1] And the views of Petras (p. 44 f.) and others are of like import. Scholars without exception seem to have blindly accepted Wright's view, with no effort whatever to test its validity.

That Wright's assumption is unwarranted, however, may be demonstrated, it is believed, beyond question. And it will be the purpose of the following pages to make good this assertion. With this end in view, we may first bring together the chief variations in incident which D exhibits.

The introduction of D contains no significant alteration of the original. A unique feature is the naming of the queen *Helie* (variant *Elye*, 223) where the French is silent, but where Y has the name *Milicent* (or *Ilacent*). In not giving a name to the prince it falls in with the French; other M. E. texts call him *Florentine*. There is a slight enlargement in the account of the meeting of the father and son, in which we have possibly a more faithful preservation of the French than in Y. Other slight variations are the additional nature-touch in having the queen ask to see the prince " In a myry mornyng of May " (261), and the requiring the sages to come to court within *three* days after the receipt of the royal message (312).

Arbor preserves all the essential motives of the French. A slight abridgment is the omission of mention of the knight's going away for the sake of " chaffare " (A, E, B, C, L).

Canis, on the other hand, contains a number of interesting variations: (1) The infant has only *two* nurses; in A, E, B, C, K, L, there are *three*,—cf. L 17, " Li enfes avoit ·iii· norrices." (2) D also fails to catalogue the duties of the nurses, which is otherwise a constant feature in both English and French (cf. Y, K, L 17). (3) A third curtailment is the complaint of the

[1] See the preface to his edition of the D-text, Percy Soc., XVI, p. LXVIII.

knight against women when he finds his child alive. (4) A very original addition is that the knight drowns himself for sorrow in a *fische-pole* in his garden (883); *L* 21 and *Y* have him go on a pilgrimage by way of atonement.

Aper exhibits comparative agreement with *Y*, except in the conclusion which has been much abridged.

The tale *medicus* is very much condensed. The ton-motif is cancelled altogether (*L* 28 f., *A* 1142 f.), and there are numerous less important omissions: *e. g.* (1) mention by name of the Earl of Navern (*Y*, *L* 27, "li quens de Namur"); (2) the cure of the invalid (*Y*, "beef's flesh," etc.; *L* 27, "char de buef"); (3) specific allusion to the prince as an *avetrol* (*L* 27, *avoltres*,—so *Y*, except *F*, *C* read *horcopp*). A single addition is that the queen of Hungary is accompanied by ten or twelve maids (1082).

Gaza. Omissions are (1) the names of both emperor and tower (*Octavian* and *Cressent*, respectively, in *A*, *Ar*, *E*, *B*, *C*, *L* 30), and (2) the warden's finding the headless body, and his endeavor to identify the same,—a feature which is preserved and worked out in detail in all other related versions (cf. *L* 32 f., *A* 1319–48).

Puteus. (1) No mention of the Roman law until late in the narrative (1413 f.); in other versions it appears at the beginning of the story (*Y*, *L* 36). (2) This law is not alluded to at all as *curfew* (cf. *L* 36, *coevre feu*). (3) The wife makes no threat of drowning herself in the well (*Y*, *L* 37). (4) The husband's excuse for being out thus late is that he thought he heard a *spangel*, which he had "mysde al thys seven-nyght" (1448-9).

Senescalcus. (1) Much abridgment of the scene between the seneschal and his wife on the former's announcing his infamous purpose. (2) Abridgment also of the early morning scene, notably the dialogue between the king and his seneschal. (3) An omitted detail is the bestowing the wife on a rich earl, which is found in *Y*, but which seems not to have been in the Old French.

Tentamina variations are (1) the wife herself contrives the "tentamina." In all the related versions, they are proposed by the mother. (2) A brother of the sage assists in the bloodletting. Omissions are (1) mention of the sage's having survived two wives (cf. *L* 43 and all M. E. versions except *F*), and (2) the wife's third visit to her mother, and the implied rôle of the parish-priest of the original and the remaining M. E. versions.

Virgilius. (1) A striking and altogether unwarranted alteration is the substitution of *Merlin* for *Vergil* (1880). (2) Allied with this is the very radical variation—probably the most radical of all in *D*—in the omission of the entire first episode, the incident of the mirror-pillars alone being preserved. Other less striking variations are (3) the two *coffers* of gold are buried, not as in the remaining M. E. versions, at the gates of the city, but in "lyttyl pyttys twaye" (1926); (4) the emperor is not asked to divide half with the brothers, nor does he accompany the latter to their place of digging, but sends one of his men with them (1932 f., 1950); (5) the brothers set fire to the foundation of the pillar before going to their inn, and even visit the emperor to bid farewell before taking final leave of the city; (6) instead of pouring molten gold down the emperor's throat, a ball of gold is ground to powder and his eyes, nose, and throat are filled with it (2067–71).

Avis. Instead of the *pie* of other texts we have a *popynjay* (2145), and (2) instead of the *maid*, a *boy* as the wife's assistant. (3) Only the boy goes on the house-top. (4) He breaks great blown bladders in imitation of thunder. (5) There is no mention of the husband's discovery of the wife's deception.

Sapientes. Important omissions are the search for, and finding of, the child Merlin and the incident, dependent thereon, of the interpretation of the dream.

Vidua. (1) An interesting invention is the husband's burial "withouten the toun at a chapel" (2484), since, in view of the manner in which he met his death, "In kyrkeʒarde men wolde hym nout delve" (2482); *A** 80, simply *au moustier*. (2)

The wife herself kindles the fire and makes her bed beside the grave (2502 f.), having first sent after her clothes (2500). (3) The knight is permitted to enter immediately on knocking; in other texts, he has to repeat his knocking and petitions. (4) The wife does not, as in other texts, propose matrimony to the knight.

Roma. (1) There are *three* heathen kings instead of *seven* as in the original (2649). (2) The page is not named till towards the end of the story, when he is called *Gynever* (2730); cf. *A** 86, *Genus; A, B, C, F, Gemes; E, B, Junyus; Ar. Julius.*

Inclusa. This story presents remarkable agreement with *Y*, the chief and only important variation being the temporary omission of the knight's explanation of the reason for his flight from his native land in that he had slain there another knight. This excuse is employed later in the story, but originates with the lady (2961).

Vaticinium. (1) The father also has the power of interpreting the language of birds (3138). (2) The name of the father is omitted (*A** 101, *K* 4919, *Girart le fils Thierri; B, C, F, Jerrard Noryes sone; E, Barnarde Norysshe*), and there is otherwise much condensation of the narrative.

Such are some of the variations of *D*. And these are doubtless what led Wright to his classification of this version. But since all these variations are peculiar to *D* they can in no way be held to confirm Wright's view. They are in fact of no value whatever in determining *D*'s relations, except in so far as they put one on guard against laying too much stress on any agreements which *D* may be found to have exclusively in common with any particular group or version.

Wright's theory, however, does seem to derive some support from another quarter, namely that *D*, in a number of instances, preserves the Old French more faithfully than any other M. E. version.[1] These are as follows: (1) In *senescalcus*, the king rules in *Apulia* (so *L* 39); in *Y*, he rules over both

---

[1] Wright, however, has not adduced any of this evidence.

Apulia and *Calabria*. (2) In *sapientes*, after all the sages have been slain and the cauldron has become clear, Merlin and Herod ride out of the city by way of testing results; the king, on reaching the gate, regains his sight (*D* 2409 f., *L* 63). Other M. E. texts omit this feature. A less significant agreement of *D* with the Old French in the same story is that the king remains blind from the time he goes outside the city gates, where *Y* represents him as being blind only when without the city, and as always recovering his sight on his return. (3) *D* 2803, *A** 89 have the knight in *inclusa* travel *three weeks* in a fruitless search for the lady of his dream. *Ar, E, C, F* have him travel three *months*,—*B, one month*.[1] (4) In *vaticinium*, the father and the son, at the beginning of the story, are on their way to visit a hermit on an island in the sea (3141 f.). This feature is suppressed in the remaining M. E. versions, but appears in all the important O. F. versions; *A** 98, "por aler à ·i· reclus qui estoit seur ·i· rochier," and *K* 4693–4, "Naiant en vont à un renclus, ki en un rochier sestoit mis." (5) In the same story (3327), the city to which the father comes in his poverty, is, in agreement with *A** 101, *Plecie* (cf. also *K* 4918, "Ales moi tost au *plaseis*,"—which Godefroy identifies with *plaisseis = clôture*). The city is not named in *Y*.

Of these agreements two (the 2d and 4th) are very significant, and serve at least to show that *D* was not based on the common original (*y*) of the six versions so far treated. They do not prove, however, that *D* goes back to the French unrelated with these, for there still remains the possibility of a connection of *D* with *y* through a common M. E. original (*x*), which *y* does not for these features faithfully reproduce. Yet it must be granted that this explanation would seem to have little in its favor could not some agreements of *D* with certain members of *Y* as against the French be shown.

[1] The Italian prose text published by Varnhagen agrees here with the M. E. versions; see p. 36, *tre mesi*.

Among these agreements are: (1) with A and C, in *canis*, in that the knight cuts out the dog's *rygge-boon* (D 859); in the French, he cuts off his head (L 20, " si li cope la teste "); (2) in *aper*, with C, in that the herd fills his *hood* with haws (D 945), A, E, B, L, his *laps;* (3) in *Virgilius*, with the entire group Y, in that there are only *two* brothers who bring about the overthrow of the image (D 1899); L 51, on the contrary, "·III· bachelers"; (4) in *vidua*, with F, A^* 84, in that the wife is called on to knock out only *two* of her husband's teeth (D 2592); according to A, Ar, E, B, C, all are knocked out; see also D^* 39, *toutes les dens;* (5) in *inclusa*, (a) with the entire group Y, in the substitution of *Hungary* for the *Monbergier* of A^* 89, K, as the land whence the knight comes (D 2787), (b) with E, F in the substitution of *Poyle* for the illogical *Hungary* of the French (A^* 89, K) as the land into which the knight finally comes (D 2805), and (c) with F in the additional detail, that the earl had been warred against for *two years* (D 2849).

But here it is possible that these agreements were accidental. Furthermore, inasmuch as the ultimate O. F. original of the M. E. versions has in all probability been lost,[1] it may be argued that those features in which D and other M. E. versions are in accord as contrasted with the Old French may have been just those in which their common original varied from the known O. F. manuscripts. Hence no final conclusion may be had from this quarter.

There remains the evidence of phraseology and of rime, and it is in this that we have a final proof of the error of Wright's assumption.

The following are some of the parallel passages revealed by a comparison of A and E with D.[2] Others might be cited, but these will suffice for the purpose.

[1] See the section devoted to a study of the source of the M. E. versions.

[2] Where A is fragmentary, E has been selected in preference to Ar, since the latter is also largely fragmentary.

D.

In Rome was an emperour,
A man of swyth mikil honur.
Is name was Deocclicius.

(1-2, 4)

Uppon his sone that was so bolde,
And was bot sevene wyntur olde.

(13-14)

The emperour for-thoght sore
Tha the child ware sette to lore.

(15-16)

Whilk of thaym he myght take
Hys sone a wyes man to make.

(23-24)

The thirde a lene man was.

(49)

And was callid Lentulus.
Hee sayed to the emperour thus.

(51-2)

And er ther passe thre and fyve,
Yf he have wyt and his on lyve,

(55-6)

And inred man he was,
And was callid Maladas.

(61-2)

The sevent mayister answerd thus,
And was hoten Marcius.

(91-2)

E.

Sum tyme þere was an Emperoure,
That ladde hys lyfe *with* moche honowre.
Hys name was Dioclician.

(3-5)

The chylde wax to ·vii· yere olde.
Wyse of speche ande dedys bolde.

(15-16)

Hys ffadyr was olde and ganne to hoore,
His sone thoo he sette to lore.

(19-20)

To hem he thought his sone take
Forto knowe the letters blacke.

(23-24)

The ·iii· mayster was a lyght man.

(51)

His name was callyd lentyllous.
He sayde a-non to the kyng.

(54-5)

Uppon payne of lemys and lyfe,
I shalle teche hym in yerys ·v·.

(59-60)

The ·iiii· mayster a redman was.
Men hym callyd Malquydras.

(61-62)

The ·vii· mayster hette Maxious,
A ryght wyse man and a vertuous.

(99-100)

D.

Evermore wil he wooke,
When on levede, anothir tooke.

(159-60)

By God, maister, I am noght dronken,
Yf the rofe his nouȝt sonken.

(209-10)

Hym byfel a harde caes.

(222)

And to have anothir wyf,
For to ledde with thy lif.

(231-2)

A.

Whan o maister him let, another him tok;
He was ever upon his bok.

(189-90)

Other ich am of wine dronke,
Other the firmament is i-sonke.

(211-2)

Ac sone hem fil a ferli cas.

(222)

Ye libbeth an a lenge lif:
Ye sholde take a gentil wif.

(227-8)

A good childe and a faire,
That sal be oure bothe ayere.
For sothe, sire, I hold hym myn,
Also wel as thou dost thyn.
(267-70)

Than sayd mayster Baucillas,
"For soth this his wondir cas:
Tharefore take counsel sone
What his best to don,
The childe answerd ther he stood,
"I wyle gyf ȝou counsel good;
Seven dayes I mot forbere
That I ne gyf no answere;
(360-3, 368-71)
I schal saue thy lyf a daye.
(381)

Thus they were at on alle,
And wenten agayen into the halle.
(388-9)
By hym that made sone and mone,
He ne hade nevere with me done.
(464-5)
"Kys me, yf thy wylle bee,
Alle my lyfe hys longe on the."
(474-5)
Callid to him a tormentour.
(509)

Also mote bytide the
As dyde the fyne appul-tre.
(582-3)

Than sayde Baucillas,
"A! sire emperour, alas!"
(688-9)

And hir clothes al to-rent,
Afte the thef wold hir have shent.

(700-1)
That knave kest hym fruyt y-nowe,
And clam a-doune fra bough to boghe.
(972-3)
And rent hys wombe with the knyf,
And bynam the bore hys lyf.
(982-3)
"A! sire," quod mayster Ancilles,
"God almighty send us pees!"
(1018-9)

Hit is thi sone, and thin air;
A wis child, and a fair.
For thi sone I tel mine,
Alse wel als tou dost thine.
(283-4, 289-90)
Than seide master Bancillas
Here is now a ferli cas!
Counseil we al herupon;
How that we mai best don.
Than seide the schild, Saunz fail,
Ich you right wil counseil,
This seven daies I n'el nowt speke;
Nowt a word of mi mowht breke;
(371-8)
I schal the waranti o dai.
(389)

With this word, thai ben alle
Departed, and comen to halle.
(401-2)
I swere bi sonne and bi mone
With me ne badde he never to done.
(451-2)
Kes me, leman, and loue me,
And I thi soget wil i-be.
(457-8)
And cleped forht a turmentour.
(498)

Ase wel mot hit like the
Als dede the pinnote tre.
(543-4)

Than seide maister Bancillas,
Sire, that were now a sori cas.
(683-4)
Th' emperour saide, I fond hire to-rent:
Hire her, and hire face i-schent;
(689-90)
He kest the bor doun hawes anowe
And com himself doun bi a bowe.
(921-2)
The herd thous with his long knif
Biraft the bor of his lif.
(933-4)
Than saide maister Ancilles,
For Godes love, sire, hold thi pes.
(977-8)

That ȝe bytyde swilk a cas	On the falle swich a cas
As bytyde Ypocras,	Als fil on Ypocras the gode clerk,
That slow hys cosyn withouten gylt.	That slow his neveu with fals werk.
(1026–8)	(994–6)
With my lorde for to play,	*With mi louerd for to plai;*
And love wax bytwen us twey.	And so he dede, mani a dai.
(1100–1)	(1083–4)
Oppon a day thay went to pleye,	So bifel upon a dai
He and hys cosyn thay twey.	He and his neveu yede to plai.
(1118–9)	(1113–4)
And mad hym myry, and spendid faste,	And beren hit hom wel on hast,
Al the wylle that hit wolde laste.	And maden hem large whiles hit last.
He that lokyd the tresour,	Amorewe aros that sinatour,
Come a day into the tour.	And sichen to-bregen his louerdes tour.
(1220–3)	(1265–8)
Bot *hastilich* smyt *of my hede.*	And *hastiliche* gird *of min heved.*
(1255)	(1299)
Byfore the dore, as I ȝow telle,	But thou me in lete, ich wille telle,
Thare was a mykyl deppe welle.	Ich wille me drenchen in the welle.
(1381–2)	(1463–4)
To do thy wyl by a-night,	Have womman to pleie aright,
Yf I schal helle the aryght.	Yif ye wil be hol aplight.
(1546–7)	(1577–8)
Now he slakys to lygge above;	Ich moste have som other love!
I wyl have another love.	Nai, dowter, for God above!
(1686–7)	(1753–4)
Er the myrrour be broght a-doune,	Who might that ymage fel adoun,
And than gyf us oure warrysoun.	He wolde him yif his warisoun.
(1906–7)	(2029–30)
And sayed, we wyte, sire emperour,	And said, al hail, sir emperour!
About this cite gret tresour.	It falleth to the to lof tresour.
(1932–3)	(2049–50)
And dolvyn a lytyl withinne the grounde,	And ther thai doluen in the gronde;
And the tresour was sone founde.	A riche forcer ther thai founde.
(1952–3)	(2079–80)
The ton sayed, sire emperour,	Than snide the elder to the emperour,
Undir the pyler that berys merour.	Under the ymage that halt the mirour.
(2002–3)	(2091–2)
Gladlich, sayed scho,	Bletheliche, sire, so mot ich the,
The bettyr yf hyt wylle bee.	So that ye wolde the better be.
(2287–8)	(2337–8)
And hadde seven clerkys wyse,	He hadde with him seven wise.
(2293)	(2343)

Who so anny swevene by nyght,
O morne when the day was bryght.
(2296-7)
The emperour and Merlyn anoon
Into the chambyr thay gonne gone;
(2339-40)
Hyt was a knyght, a riche schyreve,
That was lot hys wyf to greve.
He sate a daye by hys wyf,
And in hys honde helde a knyf.
(2471-4)
Bot sayed for non worldlys wyne
Schulde no man parte hom a-twyne.
(2487-8)
In hyr hoond scho took a stoon,
And knockyd out twa teth anoon!
(2601-2)

D.

Made to fle with hys boste
Thre kyngys and hare hoste.
(2732-3)
The knyght that met that sweven at nyght
Of that lady was so bright, ...
Ryght a lytyl fram the toure
Thare was the lady of honour,
And ate the wyndow the lady he see.
(2822-3, 2826-7, 2831)
He bytoke undyr hys hond,
And made hym stywarde of al hys londe.
Oppon a day he went to playe,
Undir the tour he made hys waye.

(2869-72)
Lenand to the mykyl toure,
To do in hys tresour.
Thorow a qweyntyse he thout to wyne
The lady that was loke there-inne.
(2895-8)

That who that mette a sweven anight,
He scholde come amorewe, aplight.
(2349-50)
The emperour him ladde anon,
Into his chaumbre of lim and ston;
(2453-4)
Sire, he saide, thou might me leue,
Hit was a knight, a riche scherreue,
So, on a dai, him and his wif
Was i-youen a newe knif;
(2563-4, 2569-70)
The leuedi saide, for no wenne,
Sche ne wolde neuer wende thenne.
(2581-2)
Than wil ich, she saide, and tok a ston,
And smot hem out euerichon.
(2713-4)

E.

And made more noyse and boste
Thenne wolde a kyng and hys hoste.
(2812-3)
And soo there come rydyng thys knyght
That had sought the lady bryghte.
He lokyd uppe into the toure,
And say that lady as white as flowre;
And anon, as he hyr say,
(2914-8)
And toke hym hys goodys in-to hys hande,
And made hym styward ouyr alle hys lande.
So oppon a day, with moche honoure,
The knyght come playnge by the toure.
(2944-7)
To make a chambyr byfore the toure
That may ben for my honoure.
Thenne thought he uppon sum quent gynne
Howe he myght to that lady wynne.
(2962-3, 2968-9)

Oppon a day stylle as stoon	The knyght toke workemen a-non,
He sent eftyr masons anoon.	And made a chambyr of lyme and ston.
(2901-2)	(2966-7)
And sate stille and made hym *glade*,	*And* bade hym ete and be *glad*,
And thus hys wyf made hym *made*.	*And* euyr he sat as he were *mad*.
(3021-2)	(3110-1)
Into Plecie when he was comen,	Amorowe the kyng thedyr came,
Ner *hys fadir hys in* was *nome*.	And *with hys fadyr hys in* he *name*.
To mete when he was redy to gon,	He and hys baronys euerychone
After hys fadir he sent anoon.	Wente to mete with hym a-non.
(3336-9)	(3473-6)

It is impossible to account for these agreements as mere coincidences, or as flowing from a translation from the same O. F. source. Some of them may indeed be, and doubtless are, due to the often stereotyped style, or the fondness for like epithets or collocations which characterize the M. E. romance; but all of them cannot be so explained. They warrant this assumption alone, that D and y are related either through the derivation of one from the other, or through a common M. E. original.

And inasmuch as D cannot have been based on y or on any of the texts which have developed from it, since in all the latter some of the O. F. features are lacking which are preserved in D,—or, conversely, y on D, in view of the very many independent variations of the latter where y is faithful to the French, we can only conclude that both y and D go back to the same lost M. E. version x.

We may accordingly sum up our results as to D as follows: (1) it is remarkably free, and exhibits many unique variations; (2) it does not represent an independent translation from the French, but is connected with at least six other M. E. versions through a common M. E. source; (3) this source was not the same as the more immediate common original of these six versions (y), but was a version one or more stages nearer the Old French.

As.—The Asloan version is at present inaccessible in the original manuscript,[1] and, as only about 200 lines of it have been printed,[2] any discussion of its relations must be very unsatisfactory. We may be permitted, however, to bring together the few facts which are known about it, and to draw from these such conclusions as their evidence may justify.

From the descriptions which have appeared, it is established that *As*, so far as it is not fragmentary, preserves the usual M. E. order of stories, but that beyond this it is, in many respects, extremely free. The names of the sages are much garbled, and they vary in the introductory enumeration from their form in the stories themselves. They are, moreover, in no case close to those of any version now in print, or to those of the remaining M. E. manuscripts.

Avis, too, the story which has been printed, exhibits very radical variation from other versions, both textually and as regards incident. There are apparent no significant agreements in rime or phraseology with any other M. E. version, while two new episodes,[3] well-known in other collections, but otherwise foreign to the *Seven Sages*, are woven into the narrative. And there are other variations, besides, such as the introduction of the wife's mother as a go-between, and mention of the burgess's name—first *Annabill*, later *Balan*.

But none of these serves to shed any light on the question of relationship. All the new features of *As*, as compared with the remaining M. E. versions and the accessible Romance versions, are peculiar to it, and hence afford no grounds for determining its connections.

[1] As already stated in my "Word of Introduction" (p. 2), Lord Talbot de Malahide declined to permit my consulting this manuscript. His reasons for doing so are, I understand, the same as those given by certain other possessors of valuable M. E. manuscripts, for which I beg to refer to Dr. Furnivall, *Temporary Pref. to the Six-Text Ed.*, Chaucer Soc., 1868, Pt. I, p. 6.

[2] In a contribution by Prof. Varnhagen (*Englische Studien*, xxv, p. 321 f.), who will edit the text for the Scottish Text Society.

[3] See *Englische Studien*, xxv, p. 322.

Prof. Varnhagen claims that *As* was made directly from some O. F. version,[1] and the lack of textual agreement between it and other M. E. versions in the story *avis* may seem to offer some support to this view,—but by no means necessarily, since it is evident that the author of *As* worked very independently.[2] And that the evidence offered by Varnhagen in support of his claim, viz., the agreement in order of stories with the O. F. *A**-type, is not adequate, he himself, I believe, will concede on reconsideration.

3. *Authorship of the Middle English Versions.*

It has been assumed in the preceding chapter that the English original (x) of the seven M. E. manuscripts A, Ar, E, B, F, C, and D, has been lost. It remains to inquire when, where, and by whom this original was made. For this purpose we unfortunately have almost no data at all, and can only resort to indirections to find directions out.

(1) For the determining the date of x the Auchinleck MS. (A) is of first importance. This manuscript dates from around the year 1330; this, then, must be the superior limit for the dating of y. And since, as has been shown, A was not derived directly from y, but rests in all probability on a lost manuscript r, which may have been based on y directly or through an intervening manuscript, and since, moreover, it is highly credible that A had already been composed some time before the Auchinleck copy was made, it is not probable that the date of y would fall later than the beginning of the fourteenth century.

And inasmuch, now, as y cannot have been this parent version, since D, though closely akin to it, was neither based immediately on it nor on any of its derivatives, but was connected with it through a common source, which source we may assume to be either identical with, or based directly on, the translation

---

[1] *Ibid.*, xxv, p. 322.

[2] *F* offers even more radical variation from other M. E. versions in some of its stories than does *As* in *avis*.

from the French, it is necessary to assign to this parent version a date before the year 1300. The year 1275 would, it is believed, represent a conservative conjecture.

(2) Available material for determining the place of translation of this parent text is somewhat more satisfactory. Of the entire group of seven versions which have been shown to be based on x, only one is in the Northern dialect, and this (C) is of comparatively late date. One other (D) belongs to the south-east Midland, while the rest (A, Ar, E, B, F) belong to the South,—a fact which well justifies the assumption that x was also Southern. Furthermore, inasmuch as three of these versions (A, Ar, E) possess marked Kentish features, and two others (B, F) show a Kentish influence, but less marked, we seem justified in a further restriction to the *eastern* South—Kent or its neighborhood—as the home of the parent text. It is further confirmatory of this view that just those versions (Ar, E) which are most faithful to x are most distinctly Kentish.[1]

(3) But while we are thus justified in indulging in conjecture as to the time and place of composition of x, in the matter of its authorship we have no grounds for such an indulgence. The nature of the subject might establish a slight probability in favor of lay authorship, but not at all necessarily; and the same is true of the references to priests, in *tentamina* and *avis*, as adulterate lovers,—especially since in the only story in which it is a constant feature (*tentamina*), it was also in the Old French; so that, in respect to this side of the problem in hand, we have, for the present at least, and probably for all time, to content us with absolute ignorance.

With regard to the authorship of the texts which have been preserved, we are equally at a loss for definite information.

An ingenious and praiseworthy effort has been made by Dr. Kölbing to demonstrate a community of authorship for the A-text and the Auchinleck texts of the *Arthur and Merlin*,

---

[1] The dialect of D—southeast Midland—also offers support to this view.

Kyng Alisaunder, and *Richard Coer de Lion*;[1] but without meaning to discredit his conclusions in general, it is necessary, we regret to say, to reject them in so far as they concern the *Seven Sages*. Kölbing's argument is made on the basis of features (rime, language, etc.) exclusively, or almost exclusively, peculiar to these poems. The only part of his argument which holds is that which concerns the expletives *cert* and *vair*. These appear only in the *A*-text, being either original with it, or, if in *y*, having been displaced in the remaining texts by other rimes. On the other hand, of the 18 rimes which Kölbing cites[2] (one of which, 2803-4, *bataille: mervaile*, should be cancelled, since it is taken from *C*), a comparison with the remaining members of *Y* shows 12 to reappear in the corresponding lines in *Ar*, 9 in *E*, etc. The evidence to which Kölbing attaches most importance, that of certain textual agreements between *Arthur and Merlin* (1201 f.) and *A* (2389 f.),[3] is likewise not valid, as is manifest from the following parallel comparison of these passages with *Ar* and *E*. Compare

'Merlin in þe strete þo pleyd,
And on of his felawes him trayd.'
(*A. M.* 1201-2).

'On a dai þai com þer Merlin pleid,
And on of his felawes him traid.'
(*A* 2389-90).

with

'So þei come þeir þe child played,
And on of his felawes hym bytrayed.'
(*Ar* 1511-2).

'Thenne come they thorowe happe there he playde,
One of his felowys hym myssayde.'
(*E* 2437-8).

Compare further, as against his citation of

'Foule schrewe fram ous go!'
'Þou hast yseyd to loude þi roun.'
Þat haþ me sougt al þis ȝer.'
(*A. M.* 1204, 18, 20).

'And cleped him schrewe faderles.'
'Al to loude þou spok þi latin.'
'Þat han me sought al fram Rcme.'
(*A* 2392, 6, 8).

---

[1] *Arthur and Merlin*, Leipzig, 1890, p. LX f.
[2] *Ibid.*, p. LXXXII.
[3] *Ibid.*, p. CIV.

the following from *Ar* and *E*:

'And clepyd hym schrewe faderlese.' 'And calde the chylde fadyrles.'
'To loude þou spake þy latyn.'
'þat haue me souȝt fro gret Rome.' 'That have sought me fro Rome.'
  (*Ar* 1514, 18, 20).   (*E* 2440, 6).

From these it is evident that any inference as to *A*'s authorship made on this basis will apply equally as well to *Ar* and *E*. Accordingly the parallels pointed out by Kölbing must either be explained as accidental, or as traceable either to an influence of *Arthur and Merlin* on the source of *A, Ar,* and *E,* or, conversely, of some one of these on the *Arthur and Merlin*.

4. *Source of the Middle English Versions.*

The question of the ultimate source of the M. E. versions has, to all intents and purposes, been settled by Petras.[1] We need only present here his general argument and his conclusion, inserting where deemed expedient additional proofs, and adding here and there details which he has omitted.

But first of all it is necessary to state that such expressions (which Petras [p. 32] inclines to accept as evidence) as *A* 2771, 'So seigh þe rime'[2] (to which add *F* 1690, 'as seyþ þe ryme') proves nothing, for by a like reasoning we might, on the basis of *Ar* 1906, 'as it saiþ in latyn,' prove a Latin source for the M. E. versions. It is not on such formulae that the presumption in favor of a metrical original of the lost M. E. original must repose; this must rather rest on the fact that

[1] See his dissertation, p. 31 f. Our investigation must differ from his, however, in that we are concerned only with the source of the parent version, *x* (*As* being disregarded), while Petras has assumed each of four versions (*A, C, F, D*) to be independent translations from the French. Since, however, he begins with the assumption that the same O. F. version was the source of all these, his argument is essentially the same as ours.

[2] References to source in the M. E. versions are numerous: *A* 317, 1245, 2766, 2770; *Ar* 1900, 1906, 2206, 2261, 2442; *E* 1253, 2779, 2784, 3445; *B* 295, 1235; *F* 928, 1683, 1690, 1973; *C* 622, 1324; *D* 1385, 1520, 2690, 2922.

this original (x) was itself in verse, and, hence probably made from a metrical text,—and that this does not permit of any definite conclusion it is hardly necessary to add.

It is not improbable, however, that this original of x was, like itself, composed of octosyllabic couplets, and it is needless to state that it was in the French language.

There exist three O. F. metrical versions,—the *Dolopathos*, the Keller text (K), and the fragmentary version C^*. The first of these, the *Dolopathos*, must, for obvious reasons, play no part in this investigation. The unique version D^* should, however, since it represents a prosing of a lost metrical version, receive equal attention with K and C^*.[1]

The only one of this group which has ever been proposed as a possible source of the M. E. versions is K; but a comparison of the two types as regards order of stories [2] reveals a considerable difference between them, only ten stories (1, 2, 4, 6, 8, 10, 11, 12, 14, 15) having the same position in each. Such a comparison, however, while bearing with it much weight, can in no wise be accepted as determining, as it would be quite natural for the redactor, or even the translator, to change about the stories at will, either with artistic purpose or with a view to making his source less apparent. Hence the safest test of relationship should be from the consideration of content, rather than of order of stories. And it is on this basis that Petras's comparison has been made. The Cotton-Auchinleck (C-A), or Weber, text he finds to contain only 460 lines which could be possible translations from the Keller text.[3] And since the latter contains over 5000 lines, it is not probable that even numerous intermediate redactions could have made such a difference. Besides this, there are many variations in incident, all which unite in making it extremely improbable that K was used by the English translator.

[1] For the *Dolopathos*, K, C^*, and D^*, see the chapter on "The Romance in France and Italy."

[2] For the order of stories in the various sub-types of the Western group, see our comparative table on page 35.

[3] See p. 33 of his dissertation.

The fragmentary text C^*, though differing somewhat from K in order of stories, seems, nevertheless, to be much nearer to it than it is to the English.

The prose version D^*, representing a lost metrical version V, exhibits still less agreement with the M. E. type, and possesses many unique features. In the content of its stories, however, it is comparatively close to K, so that in denying the claims for it, the legitimacy of any claim for D^* is also denied.

K, C^*, and D^* having been eliminated from the problem, it is necessary to conclude that the O. F. original, if metrical, has been lost. It remains to show whether or not the M. E. parent text was based on any of the prose texts which have come down to us, or, at least, which one of them nearest approximates the lost original.

The most widely known of the prose versions, the *Historia*, must be ruled out at once, since Paris has shown that the earliest date which can be given it is around the year 1330, or some time after the composition of the derivative M. E. version A. Other circumstances, such as the order of stories, the introduction of *amatores*, and the *amicus*-legend, as well as the fusion of *Roma* and *senescalcus*, together with its many modern touches, all unite in invalidating any claim for H.

The *Scala Coeli* (S) also exhibits many features at variance with the M. E. type, and its two new stories, *filia* and *noverca*, are sufficient to exclude it from the list of possibilities.

Likewise the first Leroux de Lincy (L) version, although it agrees very closely with the Middle English versions for the first eleven stories, cannot be considered their source, since it also contains the stories *filia* and *noverca*.

Nor to the *Versio Italica* does there attach any more probability, its distinguishing feature—the reversal of the order of stories—finding no parallel even in French.

There remains group A^*, or the family represented by the second text of the Leroux de Lincy edition. A presumption in favor of some member of this family is at once established in the fact that it has the same order of stories as the M. E. group. This circumstance has led Paris and others to see in this group the source of the M. E. texts, but no explicit claim has been made as to which one of the A*-manuscripts served as this original, though Petras has made a detailed investigation with a view to arriving at some definite conclusion.[1]

The results which Petras reaches,[2] however, are wholly negative. He shows in the first place that MS. 6849 [new No. 189] of the Bibliothèque Nationale, which Ellis had suggested as the probable source of the M. E. versions, is not even a possible source, but belongs to group L. He next endeavors to show that the Leroux de Lincy text of A* (the only one of the O. F. manuscripts of this type yet published) is not as close to the M. E. versions as are some of the unpublished manuscripts belonging to this family. Among the latter, he finds the MS. 4096, Laval. 13, to be nearest to the M. E. versions; thus, by way of illustration, where L, A* call the seventh sage *Merons*, this manuscript names him *Meceneus*, which approximates the M. E. *Maxencius* much more closely. Despite this fact, however, he is not willing to concede that this text was the source of the M. E. group, but maintains that the latter had its basis in a lost manuscript which is connected with the former through a common lost source.

And in this conclusion Petras is probably correct,—and assuredly so as regards the Leroux de Lincy text, as is established by certain features, which are not in A*, but which the M. E. texts have in common with K and other O. F. versions. A few of these are the following : (1) in *tentamina*, A, C read *gray bitch* = K 2604, *blanche leuriere;* L (A* 45), only *une leurière*; (2) in *Virgilius*, L (A* 51) has lost the feature of Vergil's casting images also for the east and west gates of Rome, which has been preserved in K 3960 f. and the M. E. group; (3) in *vaticinium*, the child, when discovered alone on the island, has had nothing to eat for *four* days in E, B, C,

[1] Petras, p. 37 f.   [2] *Ibid.*, p. 44.

and K 4725; A^* 99 and D^*, only *three* days. These suffice to indicate the result which would follow from a detailed comparison.

In view of this conclusion, the problem of the source of the M. E. parent text must, so far as a specific source is concerned, remain for the present unsolved. Examination of *all* A^*-manuscripts will doubtless bring us nearer to the truth, and, it is hoped, settle the question.

II (*b*.) *Sixteenth Century and Chap-book Versions.*

Under this head fall the Wynkyn de Worde version and the many chap-books founded on it, the lost Copland text, and the Rolland metrical version,—all which fall together into one distinct group apart from the M. E. group.

1. The Wynkyn de Worde text is in prose. Its date is not definitely known; in the British Museum catalogue it is entered as 1520, though Hazlitt (*Handbook*, p. 660) gives it a dating fifteen years earlier. Only one copy of the original text has been preserved, and that is imperfect. A reprint made by Gomme for the Villon Society (1885) makes the text accessible.[1]

This version seems to have been the first prose version made in English, and, as already noted, it can in no way be related with the M. E. metrical versions which antedate it. In length alone the contrast is sufficiently striking to justify a serious doubt as to any immediate relationship between them, the prose version comprising 180 pages in Gomme's edition. It is based on some member of the *Historia* family—probably a Latin[2] rather than an O. F. text. As a translation of H it

[1] *The History of the S. W. M. of Rome*, London, 1885. A few pages missing from the Wynkyn de Worde text are supplied from a chap-book version printed in 1671.

[2] Graesse enumerates a half-dozen or more prints between 1483 and 1495, any one of which may have served as the basis of this version.

is comparatively close, though it abridges at times, and also makes occasional independent additions.[1]

2. The Wynkyn de Worde edition served as the basis of a second prose edition, attributed to the printer Copland, which has been lost. The superscription to this edition, which alone has been preserved, agrees almost word for word with that of the Wynkyn de Worde edition, and it is more than probable, as Buchner suggests,[2] that it is only a reprint of it. The date of the Copland text is variously placed between 1548 and 1561.

3. The Rolland version is a very long poem written in heroic couplets, and in the Scottish dialect. The original edition bears the date 1578, but Laing has shown it to be probable that its composition dates from the year 1560. It seems to have been very popular in its day, undergoing at least five editions (1590, 1592, 1599, 1606, 1620) in little more than half a century after its first publication. A modern reprint was edited by Laing for the Bannatyne Club in 1837.

Sundry conjectures as to the source which Rolland employed have been made. Laing maintained that he used either the Copland print, or some O. F. or Latin text of *H*. Petras, who did not know of the Wynkyn de Worde version, and who makes the Rolland version his "Redaction C," investigated the question at some length,[3] and concluded in favor of the O. F. translation of *H* as Rolland's original.[4] But that neither of these views is correct, and that the Rolland text was the rather based on the Wynkyn de Worde version, has been conclusively proved by Buchner in his dissertation in the *Erlanger Beiträge*, v, p. 93 f. This he established by showing that where there are differences between the three versions—*H* (either Latin or French), the Wynkyn de Worde, and the Rolland—the last two are in almost every instance in accord

---

[1] See Buchner, *Erlang. Beitr.*, v, p. 95.
[2] *Erlang. Beitr.*, v, p. 96.   [3] See his dissertation, p. 47 f.
[4] The second text of Paris's *Deux Rédactions*. Its date is 1492.

with each other. A large number of textual parallels between the two English versions are cited in further support of this.

(4) The English chap-book versions merit but little attention. They have been numerous, but of poor quality, the later versions especially having deteriorated from the original. In some of these, new stories have been introduced, and in almost all of them the old stories have been abridged—in some of them, so as to be scarcely more than epitomes of their prototypes. That they were very popular for a long time, however, is indicated by the fact that the British Museum alone contains at least twelve various prints, one of which purports to have reached its twenty-fifth edition. Another was published at Boston in 1794,—the most recent at Warrington in 1815.

All versions of the chap-book group contain the distinctive features of *H*. They doubtless go back to the Wynkyn de Worde, or to the Copland, text.

In addition to the four versions or groups already described, there is evidence that there once existed another sixteenth century version, which, like the Copland text, has not survived. This is a dramatic version, bearing the title *The Seven Wise Masters of Rome*, which is mentioned in Henslowe's *Diary*[1] as having been made by Dekker, Chettle, Haughton, and Day, and as having been acted at London in March, 1599–1600. No later notice of its presentation has been pointed out, however, and it is altogether probable that the work was lost without undergoing publication.[2]

[1] Ed. Collier, London, 1845, pp. 165, 167. See also the *Dramatic Works of Dekker*, ed. Shepherd, London, 1873, I, p. xii.

[2] The enumeration of the late English versions should also include reference at least to the *Seven Wise Mistresses of Rome*, a chap-book modelled after the chap-book version of the *Seven Wise Masters of Rome*, and a sort of counterpart to it. The English libraries contain several versions of this type, but, though very interesting, they possess little value.

APPENDIX.

[Containing the story *medicus* according to *Ar* (1-228), with a tabulation of the corresponding lines in *A, E, B, C, F.*]

  Hys comaundement þei dide be-lyve. 152a.
  þane wex þeir̃ mochel stryve
  Be-tuen kynge and baron,
  ffor þe Emperour wold scle his son,
5 þe Emperour hym nold save.
  He lete a-none to spoile þat knaue,
  And with scourges hys body swynge;
  To foul dethe thei wold hym brynge.
  A-none after that, god it wote,[1]
10 He bade hem to hange hym fote hote.
  With scourges þei dide hym swynge,
  To foull deþe þei wold hym brynge.
  He was lade forþe with-oute pite
  þorouʒ-oute all þat fair̃ cite;
15 þeir̃ be-gan a rewfull cry
  Of many gentyll lady.
  All þe folke oute of Rome
  A-ʒeyne þat gentyll child come.
  Waleway, þei saide, with wronge
20 Schall þis child nowe be honge.
  Ryʒt a-mydward þat ilke pres
  Come rydynge Maxilles,
  And he sawe þat rewfull cas;
  Hys second master forsoþe he was
25 Hys scoler̃ to helpe and to rede
  All þe folke to hym þei bede;
  A-none to court he gan ryde,
  And with þe Emperour in reson chide
  ffonde to let þe Emperour wronge
30 þat his son be nouʒt an-hange.

[1] This line is repeated after l. 12, but is erased.

THE SEVEN SAGES.

Swyþe fast fro þe folke he rode,—
His palfray a-none to þe paleys glode:
þo come he by-forᷮ þe Emperour,
And grete hym fairᷮ with honour.
35 þe emperour by hym styll stode,
And by-helde hym with steren mode
he saide to hym, " master, þou haue
þe cors of god for techyng of þis knaue.
ȝe haue by-nome my sone his spech;
40 þe devyll of hell I þe be-tech,
Thyn felows and þou be my swyerᷮ!   152b.
ȝe schull haue lytyll hyerᷮ."
" O Syr Emperour, knyȝt of prys,
In dedes þou schold be warᷮ and wyse.
45 It is no wysdome no lyuys hale
To by-leue no womans tale.
Morᷮ to harme þane to note
A womans bolt is son schote.
ffor ȝef þou sclest hym, I be-sech
50 On þi heued fall þat ilke wrech
þat fell on Ypocras, þe good clerk,
þat sclewe his scolerᷮ þorouȝ fals werk."
" Master, I pray þe, tell þat cas
Of þat clerke Ypocras."
55 " Syrᷮ, þis tale is nouȝt lyte;
ffor ȝef þou wyllt ȝef þy son respyt,
A-for to-morowe day lyȝt,
I wyll þe tell a-none ryȝt,
A-ȝenst þe lawe, with grete wowe,
60 How Ypocras his nefew sclowe."
" I ȝeue hym respyt," said þe Emperour,
And saide anone with-oute soiourᷮ,
Mon schold a-ȝeyne feeche his son,
And put hym in-to preson.
65 þe chyld was brouȝt oute of þe ton
With well grete procession.

þo he cam to þat hall,
He a-loutede þe barons all;
And in to prison y-put he was.
70 Now tell we forþe of Ypocras.
"Syr," saide Maxillas, "paramour,
Ypocras was a clerke of grete honnour;
Of lechcraft was none his per
Neuer ʒit in þis londe her.
75 He hade with hym his nefewe
þat he schold leren of his vertue.
He saw þat child comyng of lor,
þat he nold tech hym no mor;
ffor he þouʒt, and saide also,
80 þat he in lor wold to-for hym go.
þe childe perseuyd full well, I-wis,
And hid it full wele in hert his.
His nefys herte he gan a-spye,   152c.
When he couþe all þe mastrye.
85 Ypocras gins understonde,
þorouʒ werkes of þe childes honde,
þat he couþe all his mastrye.
He bar to hym grete envye.
Sy by-fell apon a þynge,
90 Of hongre þat ilke kynge,
Hade seke a son gente;
To Ypocras a messenger sente,
þat he schold come his son to hele,
And haue he schold of gold full a male,
95 Ipocras wend ne myʒt;
He clepyd his nefewe anone ryʒt,
And bade hym wende to þat londe,
To nyme þat chylde under honde;
And whane he hade so i-do,
100 He schold come aʒeyne hym to.
þe child was set on a palfray,
And rode hym forþe on his way.

>   Þo he to þe kynge came
>   þe kynge hym by þe honde name,
> 105 And lade hym to þe seke childe.
>   Ihesus cryst to us be mylde!
>   Þat ȝonge man sawe þe childes payne,
>   He tastes his armes and his veyne;
>   He asked an urynall, as I wene,
> 110 And schewed þat uryn kenge *and* qwen,
>   Of þe childe all god it wyt,
>   And saide it was mys-by-get.
>   He gan þe qwene on side drawe,
>   And saide, "dame, a-knawe,
> 115 What man haþe by-gete þis childe?"
>   "Bel amy," scho sayde, "art þou wylde?
>   Who schold bot þe kynge?"
>   "Dame, say þou for no þynge,
>   He was neueȓ of kyngges streen."
> 120 "Lat," scho saide, "soch wordes ben;—
>   Or I schall do þe bete so,
>   Þat þou schalt neue*r* ryde noȓ go."
>   "Dame," he saide, "*with* soch tale,
>   Þy childe schall neueȓ be hale.
> 125 Tell me, dame, all þat cas,
>   How þe childe by-gete was."
>   "Bel amy, saist þou so?"
>   "Sertes, dame," he saide, "no."   152d.
>   He schoke his hede upon þe qwene,
> 130 And saide, "þouȝ þou do me to-scleyne,
>   May I nouȝt do þy childe bote,
>   Bot ȝe me tell hede *and* rote,
>   Of what man he was be-geten."
>   "No man," scho saide, "may it weten;
> 135 ffor ȝef n · counseill weȓ un-hele,
>   I schold be sclowe *with* ryȝt skyll."
>   "Dame," he saide, "so mot I the,
>   No man schall it wyt for me."

"Syr," scho saide, "it so by-fell,
140 þis oþer day in Auerell,
þe kynge of nauerne come to þis þede,
On faiʀ hors *and* in rich wede,
With my lord for to play,
And so he dide many a day.
145 I gan hym son in herte to loue,
Ouer all þynge so god aboue;
So þat for grete drewrye,
I late þe kynge be me lye;
So it was on me by-gete:
150 Syʀ, late no man þat i-wete."
"Nay, madame, for soþe, i-wys,
Bot for þat childe was gete a-mys,
He mot both drynke and ete
Contrarious drynke *and* contrarious mete,
155 ffresch beef *and* drynke þe broþe."
He ȝaf a-none þe child forsoþe.
þe childe was heled faiʀ *and* wele.
þe kynge hym ȝaf many jewell,
A wer hors i-charged with siluer *and* gold,
160 Als moch as he nyme wold.
He dide hym forþe a-none ryȝt,
And come home in þat nyȝt.
þe master hym asked ȝef he weʀ sond
"ȝa siʀ," he saide, "be seynt Symond!"
165 þo asked he, "what was his medecyne?"
He saide, "fresch beef good and fyne"
"þan was he a nauetroll."
"þou saist soþe, be my poll!"
"O," quod Ypocras, "be goddes dome!
170 þou art by-come a good grome."
þo by-gan Ypocras to þench
To scle his nefewe with some wrench.
þeiʀ-afteʀ, þe pride day, 153a
With his nefew he went to play,

175 Yn-to a faiȝ grene gardyn;
þeiȝ wex many an erbe fyn.
þe childe sawe an erbe on þe grounde,
þat was myȝty of mochell monde;
He toke it and schewed to Ypocras,
180 Bot he saide a better þeiȝ was;
For he wold þat child be-cach.
He stoupyd soch on to rech.
þo fyle Ypocras with a knyf,
He nome his nefewe of his lyf.
185 He dide hym bury unkonnynglych,
As he had dyed sodeynlych,
And afteȝ-warde, swyþe ȝerne,
He dide his bokes all to-bryne.
God of heuen, þe hyȝe kynge,
190 þat is oueȝ-seaȝ of all þynge,
Sende Ypocras for his treson,
þe foul rankkelaud menyson.
Ypocras wyst wele, for his quede,
þat he schold son be dede;
195 Bot for no þynge þat he couþe þynch
þe menyson he no myȝt quench.
A nempty ton he dide forþe fett,
And full of clene water he it pyt,
Also full to þe mouþe;
200 ffor he wold it weȝ couþe,
And dide after sende mochell and lyte,
Neȝbours hym to bysyte.
He saide to-fore hem euerchon
þat þe deþ was hym apon,
205 All with ryȝt and nouȝt with wouȝe,
ffor his nefewe þat he sclowȝe.
þat treson he gan hym reherce.
On þe tone a C. holes he gan perce.
When þe holes weȝ mad so fell,
210 He dide hem stope with dosell,

And saide to hem once or tweye,
"ʒe schall see of my mastrye."
He smered þe dosells all a-boute,
And made heme after-ward drawen oute.
215 A droþe þeir-of oute ne came;
þar-of merveiled many man.
Ypocras saide, "water y can stope,
þat it ne may uneþes drope;   153b.
But y ne may stope my menyson.
220 All it is for þat foul treson,
þat y my nefewe sclewe vylengly,
ffor he was wyser man þane y.
I nor no man under son
ʒeue me helpe ne can,—
225 Bot my nefewe o-lyue wer.
Ryʒt it is þat y mys-fair.
To soffre wo it is skyll
ffor y sclouʒ my lyuys hele."

TABLE OF CORRESPONDING LINES.[1]

Ar	A	E	B	C	F
	——	949	933	1041	——
	——	950	934	1042	——
	——	951	......	1043	——
	——	952	......	1044	——
5		953	......	(1045)	——
	——	954	......	(1046)	——
	——	955	......	(1047)	——
	——	956	......	(1048)	——
	——	(957)	——	......	(1436)
10	——	(958)	——	......	(1438)
	——	959	——	(1051)	——

[1] An identical line is indicated by an asterisk (*), an omission by a dash (——), an addition by brackets ([]), a corresponding but not similar line by leaders (......), and altered rimes by parentheses ().

THE SEVEN SAGES.

Ar	A	E	B	C	F
	—	960	—	(1052)	—
	—	961	942	1054	—
	—	962	941	1053	—
15	—	963	943	1057	—
	—	964	944	1058	—
	—	965	945	—	—
	—	966	946	—	—
	—	967	947	—	—
20	—	968	948	—	—
	963	969	949	1059	—
	964	970	950	1060	—
	966	972	952	1062	1440
	965	971	951	1061	1441
25	—	974	—	......	—
	—	973	—	......	—
	(967)	976	957*	(1065)	—
	(968)	975	958	......	—
	—	977	959	—	—
30	—	978	960	—	—
	—	979	(961)	—	—
	—	980	(962)	—	—
	969	981	963	1067	(1442)
	970	982	964	1068	(1443)
35	(971)	983	965	(1069)	(1444)
	(972)	984	966	(1070)	(1445)
	(973)	985	967	1071	(1446)
	(974)	986	968	1072	(1447)
		[87–88]	[69–70]		[48–49]
	(975)	989*	971	—	1450
40	—	990	972	—	1451*
	—	991	(973)	(1073)	(1452)
	(976)	992	(974)	(1074)	(1453)
	(977)	993	975	—	1454*
	(978)	994	976	—	1455*
	[79–88]				

Ar	A	E	B	C	F
45	989	995	(977)	——	1456
	990	996	(978)	——	1457
	992	——	——	——	1459*
	991	——	——	——	1458
	(993)	——	979	——	1460
50	(994)	——	980	(1085)	1461
	995	——	981	(1086)	1462
	996	——	982	(1087)	1463
	997	997	983	(1088)	1464
	998	998	984	……	1465
55	999	1001	985	……	(1466)
	1000	1002	986	(1091)	(1467)
	1001	1003	(987)	……	1468
	1002	1004	(988)	——	1469
	1003	1005	——	——	1470
60	1004*	1006	——	(1093)	1471
	1005	1007	989	(1094)	1472*
	1006	1008	990	——	1473
	1007*	1009	(991)	1095	1474
	1008	1010	(992)	1096	1475
65	1009	——	993	……	1476
	1010	——	994	……	1477
	——	1011	995	……	1478
	——	1012	996*	……	1479
	1011	1013	997	——	1480*
70	1012	1014	998	——	1481
	——	1017	999	1101	1482
	——	1018	1000*	1102	1483
	1014*	1019*	1001*	(1103)	1484*
	1013	1020	1002	(1104)	1485
75	1015*	(1021)	1003*	1105	1486
	1016	(1022)	1004	1106	1487
				[1107-8]	
	1017	1023	1005	1109	1488
	1018	1024	1006*	1110	1489*

THE SEVEN SAGES. 103

Ar	A	E	B	C	F
	(1019)	——	(1007)	(1111)	(1490)
80	(1020)	——	(1008)	(1112)	(1491)
	1021	1025	1009	(1113)	1492
	1022	1026	1010	(1114)	1493
	1023	1027	1011	1116	1494
	1024	1028	1012	1115	1495
85	1025	1029	1013	——	1496
	1026	1030	1014*	——	1497
	1027	1031	1015*	——	1498*
	1028	1032	1016	——	1499
	1029	1033	1017	1117	1500
90	1030	1034	1018	1118	1501
	1031	1035	1019	(1119)	1502*
	1032	1036	1020	(1120)	1503
	1033	(1037)	1021*	1121	1504*
	1034	(1038)	1022	1122	1505
95	1035	1039	(1023)	(1123)	1506
	1036	1040	(1024)	(1124) .	1507
	1037*	1041	1025	1125	1508*
	1038	1042	1026	1126	1509
	1039*	1043*	1027*	……	1510*
100	1040	1044	1028	……	1511
	1041*	1045	1029*	1129	1512*
	(1042)	1046	1030	1130	1513
	(1043)	1047	1031	(1131)	1514
	1044	1048*	1032	(1132)	1515*
105	1045	1049*	1033*	1133	1516*
	1046	1050	1034	1134	1517
	1047	1051	(1035)	1135	1519
	1048	1052	(1036)	1136	1518
	1049	1053	1037	(1137)	1520
110	1050	1054	1038	(1138)	1521
	1051	1055	1039	……	(1522)
	1052	1056	1040	……	(1523)

[41–42]

Ar	A	E	B	C	F
	1053	1057	(1041)	(1143)	(1524)
	1054	1058	(1042)	(1144)	(1525)
115	1055*	1059	1043	(1145)	(1526)
	1056	1060	1044	(1146)	(1527)
	1057	1061	1045	1147	1528
	1058	1062	1046	1148	1529
	1059*	1063	1047	1149	1530
120	1060*	1064	1048	1150	1531
	1061*	1065	1049	1151	1532
	1062*	1066	1050	1152*	1533*
	1063	(1067)	1051	(1153)	——
	1064	(1068)	1052	(1154)	——
125	1065	1069	1053*	1155	——
	1066*	1070*	1054*	1156	——
	1067 .	1071	——	1157	——
	1068	1072*	——	1158	——
	1069	1073*	——	——	1534
130	.1070	1074	——	——	1535
	1071	1075	1055	1159	1536
	1072	1076	1056	1160	1537
	1073*	1077	1057*	(1161)	1538*
	1074	1078	1058	(1162)	1539
			[59–60]		
135	1075	(1079)	(1061)	(1163)	(1540)
	1076	(1080)	(1062)	(1164)	(1541)
	1077*	1081	1063	1165	(1542)
	1078	1082	1064	1166	(1543)
	1079	1083	1065	1167	1544
140	1080	1084	1066	1168	1545
	1081	1085	1067	1169	(1546)
	1082	1086	1068	1170	(1547)
	1083*	1087	1069*	1171	1548*
	1084*	1088	1070	1172	1549
145	1085	1089	1071	1173	1550
	1086	1090	1072	1174	1551

THE SEVEN SAGES.   105

Ar	A	E	B	C	F
	1087	1091	1073	1175	1552
	1088	1092	1074	1176	1553
	1089	1093	1075	1177	1554
150	1090	1094*	1076	1178	1555
					[56-59]
	1091	1095	1077	(1179)	1560
	1092	1096	1078	(1180)	1561
	1093*	1097	1079*	1181	1562*
	1094	1098*	1080	1182	1563*
155	1095	(1099)	1081	1183	1564
	1096	(1100)	1082	1184	1565
				[85-90]	
	1097	1101	1083	1191	1566
	1098	1102	1084	1192	1567
	1099	1103	1085	1193	1568
160	1100*	1104	1086	1194	1569
	1101	(1105)	(1087)	(1195)	1570
	1102	(1106)	(1088)	(1196)	1571
	1103	1107	1089	(1197)	(1572)
	1104*	1108*	1090	(1198)	(1573)
165	1105	1109	1091	1199	1574
	1106	1110	1092	1200	1575
	1107	1111*	1093*	(1201)	(1576)
	1108	1112	1094	(1202)	(1577)
	1109	1113*	1095	1203	1578
-170	1110	1114	1096	1204	1579
	(1111)	(1115)	(1097)	(1205)	(1580)
	(1112)	(1116)	(1098)	(1206)	(1581)
	1113	1117	1099	1207	1582
	1114	1118	1100*	1208	1583
175	1115	1119*	1101	(1209)	1584*
	1116	1120	1102	(1210)	1585
	1117	1121	1103	(1211)	(1586)
	1118	1122	1104	(1212)	(1587)
	1119	1123	1105	1213	1588

Ar	A	E	B	C	F
180	1120	1124	1106	1214	1589
	1121	1125	1107	(1215)	(1590)
	1122	1126	1108	(1216)	(1591)
				[17-20]	[92-93]
	1123	1127	1109	(1221)	1594
	1124	1128	1110	(1222)	1595
185	1125	1129	1111	1223	1596
	1126	1130	1112	1224	1597
	1127	(1131)	———	———	(1598)
	1128	(1132)	———	———	(1599)
	1129	1133	1113	1225	1600
190	1130	1134	1114	1226	1601
	1131	1135*	1115*	1227	1602*
	1132	1136	1116	1228	1603
	1133	1137	1117	(1229)	———
	1134*	1138*	1118	(1230)	———
195	1135	1139	1119	1231	———
	1136	1140*	1120	1232	———
	[cf. 1142]			[33-34]	
	1143	(1141)	1121	1235	1604
	1144	(1142)	1122	1236	1605
	1145	1143	1123	———	1606
200	1146	1144	1124	———	1607
	1137	1145	(1125)	(1237)	1608
	1138	1146	(1126)	(1238)	1609
	1139	1147*	1127	1239	1610
	1140	1148	1128	1240	1611
205	1141	1149	(1129)	(1241)	(1612)
	1142*	1150	(1130)	(1242)	(1613)
	[cf. 1136]				
	1147	1151	1131	———	1614
	1148	1152	1132	———	1615
	1149	1153	1133	1243	1616
210	1150	1154	1134	1244	1617
	———	1155*	1135*	———	———

THE SEVEN SAGES.

Ar	A	E	B	C	F
		1156	1136	—	—
	1151	1157	1137*	1245	1618*
	1152	1158	1138	1246	1619
215	1153	1159*	1139	1247	1620
	1154	1160	1140*	1248	1621
	1155	1161	1141	(1249)	1622
	1156	1162	1142	(1250)	1623
	1157	1163	1143	1251	1624*
220	1158	1164	1144	1252	1625
	[59–60]			[53–54]	
	1161	1165	1145	1255	1626
	1162*	1166	1146	1256	1627
	1163*	1167	1147	—	1628
	1164	1168	1148	—	1629
225	1165*	1169	1149*	1257	1630
	1166	1170	1150	1258	1631
	—	(1172)	—	—	—
	—	(1171)	—	—	—

This partial table will serve to illustrate the correspondences between the various members of group Y. The array of figures may look repellent, but I have preferred to submit the tabulation for an entire story rather than to give only a part of it, or to resort to any printer's devices to compress it, and thereby incur the risk of impairing its value.

KILLIS CAMPBELL.

LIFE.

I was born June 11, 1872, at Enfield, King William Co., Va. My early training was acquired in the public schools of my native township. In the fall of 1888 I entered William and Mary College, where I remained for two sessions. Securing a Peabody scholarship at the University of Nashville in 1890, I entered that institution, where I remained for two years, and was graduated in 1892 with the degree B. L. In the fall of 1893 I returned to William and Mary College, and received there in June, 1894, the degree B. A. In October of the same year I entered Johns Hopkins University, where I have studied for four academic years, pursuing courses under Professors Bright and Browne in English, Professor Wood and Dr. Learned in German, and Drs. Menger, Marden, and Rambeau in French, and holding during the session 1897-98 a fellowship in English.

I take this occasion to acknowledge my obligations to all my instructors, and in particular, to Professor Bright, to whom I am deeply indebted both for guidance and encouragement in my academic work and for much valuable assistance in the preparation of this study. I wish also to thank the authorities in the British Museum, Balliol College, and Cambridge University Libraries (especially Mr. Bickley of the British Museum) for courtesies extended, and for valuable suggestions and information concerning the Middle English manuscripts of the *Seven Sages*.

KILLIS CAMPBELL.

JOHNS HOPKINS UNIVERSITY,
   May 1, 1898.

www.ingramcontent.com/pod-product-compliance
Lightning Source LLC
Chambersburg PA
CBHW020137170426
43199CB00010B/781